FV

 St. Louis Community College

Library

5801 Wilson Avenue
St. Louis, Missouri 63110

RAIN OF TROUBLES

LAURENCE PRINGLE

RAIN OF TROUBLES

The Science and Politics of Acid Rain

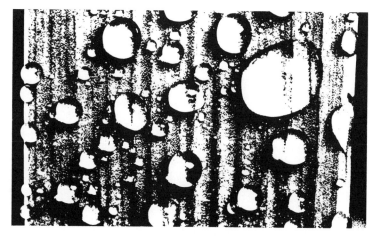

MACMILLAN PUBLISHING COMPANY
New York

COLLIER MACMILLAN PUBLISHERS
London

Dedicated to the loons, the barred
owls, and all living things in and
around Upper Sargents Pond

The author wishes to thank Ellis B. Cowling, Associate Dean
for Research, School of Forest Resources, North Carolina
State University, for reading the manuscript of this book and
helping to improve its accuracy. Dr. Cowling is a scientific
advisor in the area of forestry research to the National Acid
Precipitation Assessment Program.

Macmillan Publishing Company
866 Third Avenue, New York, NY 10022
Collier Macmillan Canada, Inc.
First Edition
Printed in the United States of America

10 9 8 7 6 5 4 3 2 1

The text of this book is set in 12 point Baskerville.

Library of Congress Cataloging-in-Publication Data
Pringle, Laurence P.
Rain of troubles: the science and politics of acid rain / by
Laurence Pringle.—1st ed.
p.   cm.   Bibliography: p.   Includes index.
Summary: Discusses the discovery, formation, transportation,
and effects on plant and animal life of acid rain and how
economic and political forces have delayed action needed to reduce
this slow poison from the sky.
ISBN 0–02–775370–0
1. Acid rain—Environmental aspects—Juvenile literature.
[1. Acid rain—Environmental aspects.] I. Title.
TD196.A25P75 1988   363.7'386—dc19   87–34950 CIP   AC

Contents

Rain
of
Troubles

People have always felt that rain is a "useful trouble," as Tennyson wrote—sometimes bothersome but life-giving, nurturing. But that feeling is changing over large parts of North America and Europe, where rain, other precipitation, and even dry particles that fall from the sky represent a chemical attack on the environment. We call this fallout acid rain, or acid deposition.

Acid rain has killed fish and other aquatic life in many lakes and streams. It harms human health, disfigures monuments and erodes buildings, and, along with other pollutants, threatens forests. It has been called "a creeping catastrophe."

The true story of acid rain resembles the plot of a science fiction movie. In the 1950s an invisible hostile force begins to attack lakes and rivers in Scandinavia, killing trout and salmon. By the 1960s it is harming the waters of eastern Canada and the northeastern United States. High-altitude forests begin to die. City statues are gradually eaten away. Damage from the alien force begins to appear in the Great Smoky Mountains, and perhaps in the Rockies, the Cascades.

Over large areas of eastern North America, people are concerned about the acidity of rain and other precipitation.

As sometimes happens in science fiction films, the authorities refuse to heed the warnings of scientists and alarmed citizens. In science fiction, however, scientists are often baffled by the alien force. Only at the last moment do they discover how to defeat the enemy. This is where an analogy between fiction and fact breaks down.

The specific sources of acid rain have been known since the 1970s. Furthermore, no "magic bullet" must be developed to halt acid rain. Methods are readily available to reduce acid deposition. Japan, Canada, and some European nations are using them to combat the menace. In the United States, however, powerful economic and political forces have blocked the widespread use of these remedies for more than a decade.

As a result, acid rain—called the environment issue of the 1980s—seems likely to continue as a threat to life on land and in waters into the 1990s. It is an unusually difficult problem that has strained relations between Canada and the United States, and pitted one region of the United States against another. As the federal government stalls and takes no action, acidic pollution continues to rain down, snuffing out the life in lakes and streams, posing a threat to other life on land. People have begun to wonder whether their leaders have the will to defeat this invisible foe.

The subtitle of this book is "The Science and Politics of Acid Rain," and you will find both aspects of the problem explored here. Chapters one through four tell how we have learned about acid deposition, how it forms and is transported, and how it affects life in water and on land. Chapters five and six tell how acid rain can be controlled, and how economic and political forces have delayed the action needed finally to reduce this slow poison from the sky.

1
Discovery

To understand the chemistry of acid rain, it helps to consider what unpolluted air is, or once was. Oxygen and nitrogen make up 99 percent of the molecules in air, but scores of other elements and compounds are naturally present. They include carbon dioxide and water, which may be in the form of gas, liquid, or solid. The unpolluted atmosphere also contains traces of methane, ammonia, sulfur dioxide, helium, and krypton, as well as particles of dust picked up by the wind, especially over deserts and plains.

Natural events can temporarily alter the chemistry of large air masses that make up the atmosphere. When a drought produces unusually dry soil conditions, greater amounts of dust particles are carried aloft. Dust tends to neutralize acids in the air. So does ammonia that arises from the process of decaying vegetation. Giant forest fires spew numerous chemical compounds into the air, including many tons of carbon dioxide. This may briefly change the chemistry downwind, as some of the carbon dioxide changes to the rather weak carbonic acid (the chemical that produces the fizz in carbonated soft drinks).

Volcanoes can also alter air chemistry. The 1982 erup-

Volcanic eruptions are a natural source of sulfur dioxide, but contribute much less to acid rain than human activities do.

tion of Mexico's El Chichon volcano sent an estimated
20 million tons of sulfur dioxide into the upper atmosphere. Sulfur dioxide reacts with other elements to
form sulfuric acid, so volcanoes are a source of acid rain.
However, their acidic emissions are brief and cause only
small increases in acidic deposits as compared to the
acid rain caused by humans.

Unpolluted rainwater tends to be slightly acidic. We
know this partly as a result of analysis of snow that fell
on Greenland more than 180 years ago. Cores of glacial
ice reveal that Greenland snow in the early 1800s had
little or no acidity. It measured between 6 and 7.6 on
the pH scale—the common measure of the relative acidity or alkalinity of matter. (The term *pH* stands for "potential Hydrogen"; see "About pH," below.) The pH
scale runs from 0 to 14, with numbers close to 0 highly

ABOUT pH

The term *pH* stands for potential Hydrogen, and
is a measure of the number of positively charged
Hydrogen ions (H^+) concentrated in a substance,
in contrast to its negatively charged hydroxyl ions
(OH^-). An ion is an electrically charged particle;
positive ions are called cations, negative ones, an-
ions. When a substance such as water contains equal
numbers of hydrogen and hydroxyl ions, its pH is
neutral. As its hydrogen ions increase, so does its
acidity. Simply defined, an acid is a substance ca-
pable of *providing* hydrogen ions for chemical reaction. A base is a substance that *accepts* hydrogen
ions.

---

acidic and those close to 14 the most alkaline. The scale is also logarithmic, so each change of one pH unit represents a chemical change of ten times. In other words,

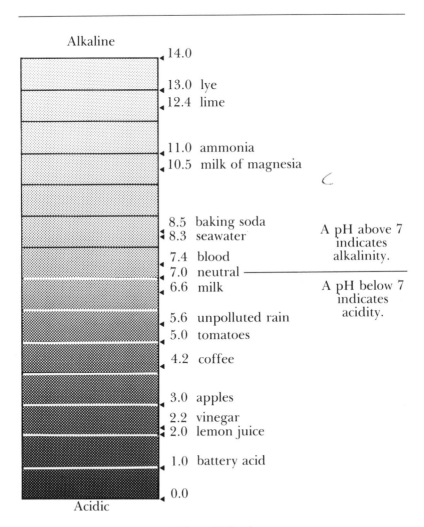

Alkaline

14.0

13.0 lye
12.4 lime

11.0 ammonia
10.5 milk of magnesia

8.5 baking soda
8.3 seawater

7.4 blood
7.0 neutral
6.6 milk

5.6 unpolluted rain
5.0 tomatoes

4.2 coffee

3.0 apples
2.2 vinegar
2.0 lemon juice

1.0 battery acid

0.0
Acidic

A pH above 7 indicates alkalinity.

A pH below 7 indicates acidity.

The pH Scale

pH 4 is ten times more acidic than pH 5, and pH 3 is one hundred times (ten times ten) more acidic than pH 5.

The acid in automobile batteries measures about 1 on the pH scale. Concentrated lemon juice has a pH of about 2, vinegar about 2.2. Pure, distilled water has a pH of 7—it is neutral, neither acid nor alkaline. With a pH of 8.5, baking soda is alkaline but not nearly as strong as the chemical called lye (sometimes used in soap making) with its pH of 13.

Beginning in the late nineteenth century, snow deposited in Greenland's glaciers became more acidic as a result of industrialization in the Northern Hemisphere. Coal was the main fuel of many industries, and coal contains sulfur. Coal burning produces sulfur dioxide, which in the atmosphere may be converted to sulfuric acid.

In 1872 British chemist Robert Angus Smith studied the heavily polluted air of London and coined the term acid rain. In his book *Air and Rain: The Beginnings of a Chemical Climatology*, Smith wrote, "Acidity is caused almost entirely by sulphuric acid, which may come from coal or the oxidation of sulphur compounds from decomposition. . . . The presence of free sulphuric acid in the air sufficiently explains the fading of colours in prints and dyed goods, the rusting of metals, and the rotting of blinds." Smith also noted that acid rain eroded the stone of buildings, particularly in the lower parts where rainwater accumulated. His observations were sound but were largely ignored.

Eighty years passed before another scientist, Eville Gorham, investigated the phenomenon of acid rain.

Gorham stumbled upon it by accident, while studying the ecology of peat bogs in the 1950s. In order to understand the nutrition of bog plants in England's Lake District, he began to collect and analyze rainwater. "The minute I started analysing the rain," he recalled, "I found that we were alternately dosed with sea salt when the winds blew from the Irish Sea and with acid from the winds that blew up from industrial Lancaster."

Like Robert Angus Smith's book, the research of Eville Gorham caused no concern when he published his findings in 1955. This was before the 1962 publication of Rachel Carson's *Silent Spring*, before the birth of the environmental movement, before the public became conscious of the harmful side effects of technological developments. Scientists were, however, starting to study the chemical composition of the atmosphere.

Even before Gorham began his work, agricultural scientists had set up a rain-sampling network in Europe. Their goal was to discover what chemicals were in precipitation, in order to discover whether airborne chemicals actually fertilized crops. Precipitation was collected at more than a hundred stations in northern and western Europe, and the data gave a record of changes in pH over that region.

In 1961 a Swedish scientist named Svante Odén began to collect water samples from lakes and rivers. After a few years he saw a clear connection between changes in the chemistry of these surface waters and those in the chemistry of rain collected in the European sampling network. The rainfall over northern Europe had become more acidic. And as the acidity of precipitation increased, so did the acidity of Scandinavian lakes and rivers. This increase coincided with increased burning of coal and other fossil fuels in central Europe and Great Britain.

In the spring of 1967 Odén received a call from a fisheries inspector who told of Swedish lakes in which fish were dying and others in which they had disappeared. The pH measurements of the lakes seemed much lower than normal. Could there be a connection?

Acid deposition can kill fish directly, or kill them indirectly by reducing their food supply or preventing successful reproduction.

This was the first known consequence of the acidic conditions Odén had found in surface waters. Odén recalls, "I was shocked to realize that we were already in a situation where damaging effects could be demonstrated. This made the problem of acid rain a real problem for the first time."

The decline of fish and other aquatic life in Sweden and Norway had actually been under way for decades. Unexplained kills of Atlantic salmon had been reported as early as 1911. Brown trout began disappearing from mountain lakes in the 1920s and 1930s. By the 1950s many lakes in southern Norway were lifeless, but no one could explain these losses. Svante Odén was the first person to link this damage to pollutants carried long distances by air. He also raised questions about other possible effects of acid rain—on soils, forest trees, and other plants. When his findings were published in 1968, the menace of acid rain, first described by Smith in 1872, finally caught public and scientific attention.

The Swedish government began its own study of acid precipitation and presented the results at the 1972 United Nations Conference on the Human Environment, held in Stockholm. This international conference was an apt forum at which to present the Swedish report entitled "Air Pollution across National Boundaries." Seventy-seven percent of the acid precipitation falling on southern Sweden came from other countries—a "form of unpremeditated chemical warfare."

Sweden's report also warned that acid precipitation might be affecting parts of Canada and the northeastern United States. Neither nation, however, had a network of stations where precipitation was collected and ana-

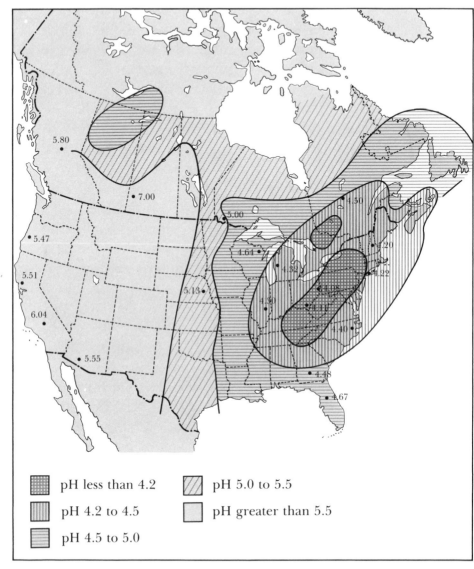

This map shows the acidity of precipitation that was recorded in 1980. The numbers vary somewhat from year to year, but the distribution pattern stays about the same.

lyzed. Few data were available to show how the acidity of rain might have changed over decades in North America.

Among the earliest measurements of precipitation pH in the United States were those made in 1939, in the state of Maine. The pH was 5.9—the slightly acidic condition of unpolluted rain. Between 1959 and 1966, agencies of the United States government took monthly precipitation samples across the nation. Chemists commonly found pH values above 6.5 west of the Mississippi, with much more acidic readings in the East. Not until the mid-1970s, however, did the United States and Canada set up a long-term program for studying the chemistry of precipitation.

Ecologists studying nutrients in a New Hampshire forest were the first to become aware of acid rain in the United States. In 1964, Gene Likens, then of Cornell University, F. Herbert Bormann of Yale University, and Noye Johnson of Dartmouth College began measuring the pH of rain and snow at Hubbard Brook Experimental Forest in New Hampshire. Between 1965 and 1971 the average pH ranged between 4.03 and 4.19— more than ten times as acidic as normal precipitation. In 1969 Gene Likens visited Sweden, met Svante Odén, and learned how acidic precipitation was affecting aquatic life there.

The findings of Likens and his colleagues were first published in the March 1972 issue of the journal *Environment*. The article summarized the data and effects of acid rain in Scandinavia, then linked these with what was then known about North America: "The eastern U.S., particularly New England, undoubtedly receives sulfur and nitrogen oxides from the West and Midwest, but large-scale changes and effects associated with increased inputs of these compounds and increased acidity of precipitation have been largely overlooked or ignored. . . . Data collected on atmospheric pollution and acid rain suggest a very serious problem in northern Europe. Existing data suggest that the problem in the United States, particularly in the Northeast, has already reached similar proportions. We urge . . . a massive effort to increase our understanding of this problem."

2
Where
the
Winds
Blow

Since 1972, when Gene Likens called for a massive effort to understand the problem, hundreds of millions of dollars have been spent on acid rain research. To an unusual degree, the search for knowledge has been used by those opposed to acid rain controls as an excuse for delay. However, as Gene Likens himself said in 1986, "As a scientist I want to know more about complexity, but more information is not needed for regulation. We know a lot already."

The term acid rain *sounds* simple, but it represents great complexity and is misleading in itself. First, some acidic compounds do not form until *after* they reach the ground or vegetation. And acids arrive in all kinds of weather—not only in rain, but also in snow, sleet, fog, on hazy and clear days or nights. In other words, all of the time. That is why scientists refer to acid deposition, a term used frequently in this book as a reminder that acid fallout can be wet or dry.

The smallest source of acid deposition—less than 5

percent—is natural phenomena, such as volcanic eruptions, decaying vegetation, and sea spray. More than 95
percent of acid rain comes from human sources, and
most of that originates wherever fossil fuels (coal, oil,
natural gas) are burned. The sources include electric
power plants, ore smelters, steel mills and other industries, and the engines of automobiles and other gasoline-
powered vehicles. The single greatest source in the
United States is coal-fired power plants.

When a fuel is burned, the sulfur in it combines with
oxygen in the air to form sulfur dioxide. It is the chemical forerunner, or precursor, of sulfuric acid, also called
acid sulfate. Nitrogen from the air itself and from burning fuels combines with oxygen to form either of two
nitrogen oxide compounds. Nitrogen oxides are the
precursors of nitric acid, also called acid nitrate. (See
"More About Acid Rain," below.)

MORE ABOUT ACID RAIN

Sulfur (S) and nitrogen (N) from burning fuels
combine with oxygen (O) to form sulfur dioxide
(SO_2) and nitrogen oxides—either nitric oxide
(NO) or nitrogen dioxide (NO_2). In the atmosphere, the sulfur dioxide and nitrogen oxides may
combine with water (H_2O) to form acids:

$$SO_2 + \tfrac{1}{2} O_2 + H_2O \rightarrow 2H^+ + SO_4^=$$
$$NO + NO_2 + O_2 + H_2O \rightarrow 2H^+ + 2NO_3^-$$

Direct reaction with oxygen is just one way in
which sulfur dioxide and nitrogen oxides become
acid sulfate and acid nitrate. Acids may also form
as a result of interaction with other compounds that

contain oxygen: ozone (O), hydrogen peroxide (H_2O_2), and the hydroxyl radical (OH). Hydroxyl radicals react so quickly with other compounds that their concentration in air is low, but atmospheric chemists believe they play an important role in the formation of acids. One source of hydroxyl radicals is a reaction of ozone and water:

$$O + H_2O \rightarrow 2HO$$

The hydroxyl radical can react with sulfur dioxide to form a bisulfite radical:

$$SO_2 + OH \rightarrow HSO_3$$

The bisulfite radical then combines with water to form acid sulfate:

$$HSO_3 + H_2O \rightarrow H_2SO_4 + H^+$$

In the atmosphere, nitrogen oxides usually change to nitric acid within hours. The conversion of sulfur dioxide to acid sulfate may take longer, up to several days, and occurs fastest in summer sunlight. Both kinds of acids may fall to earth either on small particles or in solution on raindrops or other precipitation.

Acids in precipitation are relatively easy to measure. Dry deposition is difficult to measure, although collecting devices have been improved. As recently as 1979, scientists in southern California learned that about twenty times more acid reaches the ground in dry form than in rainfall. Precipitation is scarce there, but that doesn't stop acids from "raining" down. Some fall as tiny particles, some as gas that is taken in directly by plant leaves or dissolves in lakes or in moisture on vegetation or in the soil. (See "Wet or Dry Acids," below.) Dry deposition is naturally greatest in arid regions. In areas that have plentiful rain, precipitation brings the heaviest doses of acid. The Hubbard Brook Watershed in New Hampshire receives two-thirds of its acid sulfate in precipitation, one-third in dry form.

The rain or snow at the beginning of a storm is usually most acidic, as acidic compounds or their precursors are washed from the clouds. Rain is also more strongly acidic in the summertime. Typically, summer high-pressure systems move slowly from west to east, allowing plenty of time for acids to form. Just one summer thunderstorm can flush a heavy dose of these acids out of the sky.

WET OR DRY ACIDS

Acid deposition consists of compounds that are acidic when they fall to the earth's surface in wet or dry form, as well as compounds that react with water in soil or on vegetation or other substances and become acids. Sulfuric acid dissolved in water consists of sulfate ions ($SO_4^=$) and hydrogen ions (H^+). Dissolved nitric acid consists of nitrate ions (NO_3^-) and hydrogen ions (H^+). Since sulfuric acid releases two hydrogen ions per molecule, whereas nitric acid releases one, sulfuric acid contributes more acidity to the environment. (Also, in North America and the rest of the world, more sulfur dioxide than nitrogen oxides is emitted into the atmosphere.)

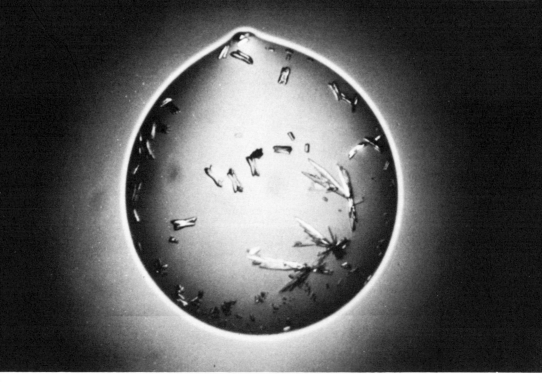

When ash particles from a power plant are injected into a water droplet exposed to sulfur dioxide (above), acid sulfate crystals form. The enlargement below shows the round ash particles and needle-like sulfate crystals within the droplet.

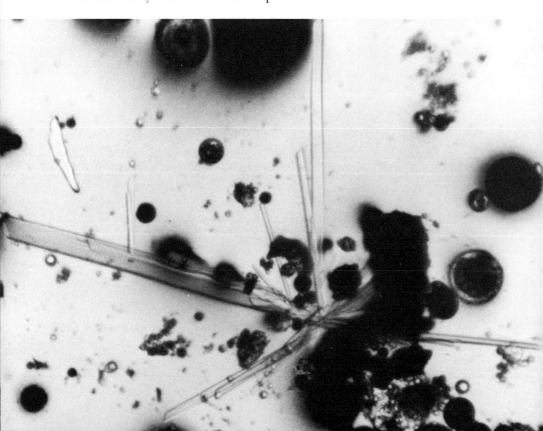

Atmospheric chemists say there are many unanswered questions about what occurs in the chemical soup of our polluted atmosphere. Some compounds are catalysts; others inhibit reactions. The chemistry of the air changes with the time of day, wind speed and direction, season, and other factors. Nevertheless, there is one unavoidable fact: What goes up comes down. There is a direct relationship between the amounts of sulfur dioxide and nitrogen oxides emitted and the acids that eventually fall to earth.

Most scientists agree that sulfur dioxide is responsible

Power plants that burn fossil fuels produce about two-thirds of sulfur dioxide emissions in the United States.

for about two-thirds of the acid rain in the eastern United States and Canada. West of the Mississippi, nitrogen oxides play a greater role. Around cities in southern California, more nitric acid than sulfuric acid falls from the sky because in that area automobiles contribute more pollutants than power plants.

In the mid-1980s the United States discharged about 26 million tons of sulfur dioxide into the atmosphere each year. Of this, 66 percent came from coal-fired and oil-fired power plants. Smelters, refineries, and other industries added 26 percent, while fuel burning in businesses, homes, and vehicles contributed 8 percent.

In that same period, about 23 million tons of nitrogen oxides also spewed into the air each year in the United States. Power plants emitted 330 percent; transportation, 40 percent; industries, 25 percent; and homes and other sources, 5 percent. Cars, trains, and other forms of transportation were expected to remain the leading source of nitrogen oxides, but the share produced by power plants was projected to reach 36 percent by the year 2000.

Canada in the mid-1980s contributed another 5 million tons of sulfur dioxide and 2 million tons of nitrogen oxides. The Canadian emissions began to decline, however, as a result of a control program launched in 1985.

For decades the number one source of sulfur dioxide in North America has been the huge Inco, Limited, copper and nickel smelter in Sudbury, Ontario. Each year the Sudbury plant alone discharged 1 percent of all airborne sulfate in the world (including both natural and human sources). Operating at full capacity, the plant emitted 3,400 tons of sulfur dioxide a day.

In the 1960s pollutants from the smelter killed many trees and other vegetation, creating a sort of barren moonscape downwind from the plant. In 1970 the province of Ontario ordered Inco to reduce emissions. Some control steps were taken, but the air of Sudbury remained unhealthy. The company claimed it could not afford the cost of more-effective controls, and the government approved another "solution": building the world's tallest chimney.

At 1,250 feet, Superstack (as it is called) is almost as tall as the Empire State Building. On its completion in the early 1970s, sulfur dioxide levels near the smelter dropped dramatically. The local air quality improved, and plant life began to grow again. Sudbury residents could see and smell an improvement in the air. But all of those thousands of tons of sulfur dioxide had not disappeared. High overhead, waste gases continued to spew out of Superstack. The sulfur dioxide was being carried wherever the winds blew.

Tall smokestacks were also seen as a remedy for air pollution in the United States. The Clean Air Act of 1970 established limits for certain pollutants. The standards were aimed primarily at protecting human health, and were based on measurements of air near the ground that could actually be breathed by people—ambient air. If ground-level concentrations were too high, the Environmental Protection Agency (EPA) or a state pollution-control agency would seek to identify the pollutant's source. The polluter could then be required to decrease the amounts of sulfur dioxide, ozone, or other wastes being emitted into the air.

Rather than install costly pollution controls, the operators of many coal-burning electric power plants built tall smokestacks that dispersed pollutants well above ground level. This was done with the full approval of the EPA and state air pollution regulatory agencies. The pollutants were just being shipped elsewhere, but this wasn't widely known or understood at the time.

In 1973 a large midwestern coal-burning utility, American Electric Power, boasted in advertisements of being a pioneer in the use of tall smokestacks to "disperse gaseous emissions widely in the atmosphere so that ground level concentrations would not be harmful to human health or property." Furthermore, the utility claimed that gases "are dissipated high in the atmosphere, dispersed over a wide area and come down finally in harmless traces."

By 1975 several dozen tall stacks had been built in the United States—many between 600 and 880 feet, several higher than a thousand feet. A decade later an estimated two-thirds of all surfur dioxide discharged annually in the United States spewed from power plants with tall stacks. These huge chimneys eased local pollution problems but sent wastes to other regions, across state boundaries and into Canada.

Many factors influence the fate of chemicals once they emerge from a smokestack. Pollutants emitted just before or during a rainstorm or snowstorm quickly fall to earth with the precipitation. Under some circumstances, most pollutants remain in the "'mixing layer" of the atmosphere. This zone of air, about 3,000 feet high on summer days, usually has good vertical mixing of gases. Pollutants trapped in the mixing layer tend to reach the ground close to their sources.

The Top 25 Sources of Sulfur Dioxide
Emissions in the United States and Canada

Rank	Plant Name	State or Province	Emissions in Kilotons per Year
1	Inco	Ontario	807.5
2	Noranda	Quebec	537.5
3	Paradise	Kentucky	418.8
4	Inco	Manitoba	333.5
5	Muskingum River	Ohio	306.7
6	Gavin	Ohio	297.5
7	Cumberland	Indiana	296.2
8	Clifty Creek	Indiana	295.3
9	Baldwin	Illinois	237.2
10	Monroe	Michigan	224.3
11	Labadie	Missouri	222.6
12	Kyger Creek	Ohio	219.7
13	Harrison	West Virginia	215.1
14	Johnsonville	Tennessee	188.0
15	Mitchell	West Virginia	187.3
16	Hatfield Ferry	Pennsylvania	173.5
17	Eastlake	Ohio	172.8
18	Bowen	Georgia	170.3
19	Lambton Generating Station	Ontario	160.3
20	Gibson	Indiana	187.8
21	Nanticoke Generating Station	Ontario	155.1
22	Hudson Bay Mining & Smelting	Manitoba	152.0
23	Conesville	Ohio	151.8
24	Shawnee	Kentucky	146.1
25	Algoma Steel	Ontario	143.3

Compiled by agencies of the U.S. and Canadian governments in 1980, this ranking of ore smelters and coal-burning power plants changed very little in the following decade.

Cool temperatures, however, cause the mixing zone to narrow or to disappear completely. In the winter the mixing layer is rarely as high as a tall smokestack. So in winter and on cool nights during the rest of the year, pollutants from tall stacks spew up beyond the mixing layer. But even during warm summer days, the hot gases erupting from tall smokestacks at fifty miles an hour can usually pierce the mixing layer. Once beyond it, the gases join the air masses of major weather systems, where strong winds can carry acid precursors hundreds of miles.

Long-range transport of pollutants is not a modern discovery. Red dust from the Sahara fell on Britain in 1755. Europeans smelled smoke from a huge Canadian forest fire in 1950. Currently, storms coming from the eastern United States carry highly acidic rain to Bermuda, 600 miles offshore.

One of the most troublesome puzzles about acid deposition is the connection between source and receptor. We know that acids fall to earth in some places (receptors), but how do we find exactly where the acids come from (sources)? Source-receptor relationships have been the subject of many studies. In 1986 the Center for Environmental Education, Inc., sponsored an entire conference focused on this aspect of acid rain research. Source-receptor studies spark plenty of interest and controversy because they have the potential of fixing blame on polluters.

There are two basic ways to link source and receptor: to study weather patterns and trace a particular fall of acids back to its source, or to somehow connect acid precursors from a specific source with a distant receptor area. Neither method yields data as precise as scientists would like because of the vastness and complexity of our ocean of air, and the difficulty and cost of conducting this sort of research.

To trace acids to their source, scientists use satellite photographs of storms and such weather data as wind speed and direction in order to follow a weather system backward in time. Using this method, highly acidic rain (pH 3.9 or less) in central Massachusetts was traced to the Ohio Valley and other midwestern sites where coal-fired power plants are concentrated. Most of the sulfuric and nitric acids falling in south central Ontario, Canada, were also traced to the midwestern United States. Infrequent but strong doses of acid precipitation in Massachusetts were traced to the Sudbury, Ontario, ore smelter site.

Satellite photos reveal the paths of weather systems and help scientists trace acidic deposits back to their general sources.

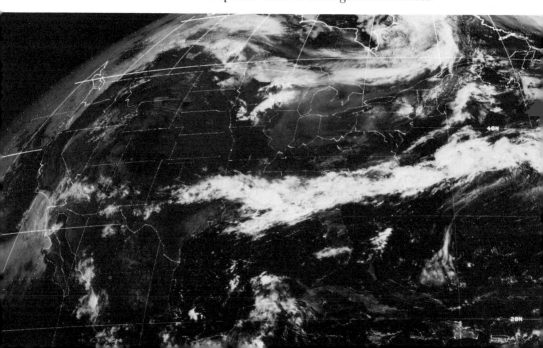

Air samples collected atop the Adirondacks' Whiteface Mountain commonly contain acids from midwestern coal-burning power plants.

The Adirondack Mountains of New York State, an area hard-hit by acid deposition, have been the site of several source-receptor studies. In one year-long study, researchers found that just 5 percent of the sulfuric acid falling on Whiteface Mountain in the central Adirondacks came from northeast storms. Twenty-five percent came from the Sudbury area, and 62 percent from weather systems that had passed through the Midwest. Much more nitric acid also reaches the Adirondacks from the Midwest than from the Northeast.

In the second method of studying source-receptor relations, scientists attempt to connect certain elements in air masses to their sources several hundred miles away. Meteorologist Kenneth Rahn of the University of Rhode Island and his assistant, Douglas Lowenthal, applied this method to samples of air collected at many sites in New England.

They knew that combustion of different types of fuel produces different elements and, equally important, that there are regional differences in the types of fuel burned. For example, most power plants along the East Coast burn a fuel called heavy residual oil. It produces nickel and vanadium that can be detected in air samples far from the power plants. Coal, the main fuel of midwestern power plants, contains little nickel or vanadium but gives off selenium and arsenic. Copper and nickel smelters, such as the Inco plant at Sudbury, emit iridium.

Such elements, according to Rahn and Lowenthal, give a kind of chemical signature to an air mass that contains emissions from a specific region. They analyzed the chemistry of air samples and recorded the amounts of different elements. Then they looked to see whether the chemical patterns matched weather patterns. In most cases they found that the chemical and weather evidence agreed "in terms of where the pollution was coming from on any given day."

They concluded that some locally produced pollution was always present. At sites in Rhode Island and Vermont, the elements revealed that pollution was mostly local about half the time. The rest of the time, it came from the Midwest, when large air masses brought the elements commonly produced by coal-burning power plants.

In New York's Adirondack Mountains, an area hard-hit by acid deposition, biologists collect information about acidity and aquatic life in scores of lakes. Llamas are sometimes used as pack animals in the most remote areas of the Adirondacks.

Their findings were based on chemical analysis of air samples taken near the ground, not of rain or snow that usually brings down the strongest doses of acid. This method of linking source and receptor also didn't give a measure of the *amounts* of acidity deposited from different sources.

Other kinds of tracers have been used to track specific air masses. Several times in the fall of 1983 a special inert gas, which had been produced in a laboratory, was released from Dayton, Ohio, or Sudbury, Ontario. Then researchers from the United States and Canada followed the paths of the gas. Each time, the gas was detected in thousands of air samples, some of which were collected by aircraft that flew across the path of the air mass that carried the gas.

The gas was found in samples collected in Vermont and New Hampshire, more than 600 miles from a release site in Ohio. One dose of the gas from Ohio was released into light winds; this produced a broad distribution pattern that extended from New Hampshire to New Jersey. Another Ohio release was whisked rapidly eastward in a narrow plume across Pennsylvania and New Jersey. A release from Sudbury traveled slowly southward and then stalled for several days over central Pennsylvania. In yet another release from Ohio, the air mass containing the tracer gas passed *over* another stable air mass, then touched down in central New York; the highest concentrations of the gas were recorded in Vermont.

The air sampling for this project was based on a computer model that predicted the likely path of each release of the tracer gas. Other computer models have been used to tie sources to receptors. The most sophisticated models include data on smokestack height, wind speed and direction, and even the amount of sunlight (which influences acid sulfate formation). However, computer models cannot take all meteorological factors into consideration. A model that agrees well with actual field data in one season or one year may be less accurate another time, as a result of variations in the weather patterns.

Further research using computer models for pollutant tracing is planned, in order to better understand the relationship between sources and receptors. More can be learned, but there are really no mysteries at all about the main sources of acid rain or the areas that get the worst of acid deposition. Knowledge about *general* source-receptor relationships is already sufficient for steps to be taken against acid rain.

3
Deadly
Waters

An umbrella in tatters, partly eaten away by acid rain—
this is a favorite image of editorial cartoonists. If the
effects of acid rain were that immediate and personal,
people would have acted swiftly to end such pollution.
Instead, the effects are subtle and affect most people
indirectly. The harm is real, however, and well docu-
mented by studies of lakes, ponds, and streams.

Although rain falls everywhere, the amounts of acid
deposition vary, and all waters are not equally vulnerable to acidification. New York's Adirondack Mountains
offer an example: Three lakes that lie within twenty
miles of each other receive precipitation of the same
acidity, yet each has a different pH measurement.
Panther Lake has a neutral pH of 7, Lake Sagamore has
a slightly acidic pH of 5.8, and Woods Lake has a pH
of about 4.5. Woods Lake no longer supports fish, frogs,
or other aquatic animals.

How can these lakes be so different? The answer lies
in their watersheds, the area from which each lake receives its water. It also lies within the lakes, in the rocks,
soils, and vegetation underwater. Each lake and its watershed differs in its ability to neutralize acids. This is
called its acid neutralizing capacity.

Research has revealed that shallow soils in the watershed of Woods Lake have low acid neutralizing capacity, so the lake's aquatic life has been nearly wiped out by acid deposition.

This vital characteristic can be demonstrated by putting a teaspoon of baking soda in the bottom of a cup, which represents the basin of a lake. Then pour a quarter teaspoon of vinegar (pH 2.2) over the baking soda (pH 8.5). In the bubbling reaction, all of the vinegar molecules react with baking soda molecules, and the vinegar and soda are broken apart. All of the acidic vinegar is neutralized. Most of the baking soda remains, however, so the basin still has considerable acid neutralizing capacity.

If just a pinch of baking soda were present in the cup, however, it would not neutralize a quarter teaspoon or more of vinegar. Some vinegar would remain; the basin's acid neutralizing capacity would be exhausted.

These simple demonstrations do not, of course, represent the complexity of nature. In lake watersheds, natural processes produce alkaline compounds and replenish their acid neutralizing capacity. Even with this replenishment, however, the acid neutralizing capacity of many watersheds is overwhelmed by acid deposition.

A lake's acid neutralizing capacity depends mainly on the bedrock geology of its watershed. Some watersheds are made up largely of such rocks as granite, quartzite, and quartz sandstone that resist weathering and are often covered by only a thin layer of soil. Neither the rocks, soils, nor waters contain many carbonates, bicarbonates, or hydroxides—alkaline compounds that neutralize acids. Regions with this kind of geology are especially vulnerable to acid rain.

Although granite bedrock has low acid neutralizing capacity, soil deposits over such bedrock can effectively neutralize acids. This explains the differing acidity of Panther, Sagamore, and Woods lakes in the Adirondacks. The soil around neutral Panther Lake is, on the average, eight times deeper than that surrounding acidic Woods Lake. Lake Sagamore has a mixture of shallow and deep soils in its large watershed, so it, too, is better able to neutralize acids than the Woods Lake watershed.

The midwestern United States has deep soil deposits and bedrock of limestone and dolomite that provide great acid neutralizing capacity. There is irony here— if the acids emitted from midwestern power plants spewed out of *short* smokestacks, they would soon settle onto lands and waters that could easily neutralize the acids. According to one EPA official, "There isn't enough coal in the world to acidify those waters."

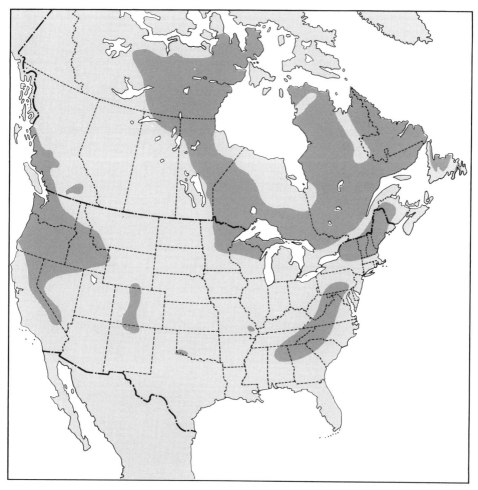

Lakes and streams found in the shaded areas on this map of North America are most vulnerable to acid deposition, because the bedrock of these areas has low acid neutralizing capacity.

But from the Midwest and its mostly alkaline soils, prevailing winds carry acid pollutants to regions that are low in acid neutralizing capacity. These include much of the Northeast and parts of the Appalachians, the Great Smoky Mountains, and southern states. Other areas in the United States that are particularly acid

sensitive are northeastern Minnesota, parts of northern
Wisconsin and northern Michigan, parts of the Rocky
Mountains, the Sierra Nevada, and the Pacific North-
west. Vast areas of central and eastern Canada, including Nova Scotia, also have bedrock that has little capacity
to neutralize acids. In all, more than 1.5 million square
miles of North America have little defense against acid
deposition.

Mountainous areas receive the heaviest doses of acid
rain, especially on their western slopes. When an air
mass meets highlands, it is forced to rise. Higher in the
atmosphere it is under less pressure and expands. The
heat of the air mass also expands, so the air cools. This
process causes clouds to form and precipitation to fall
more frequently over mountains than over lowlands.

Late winter and early spring thaws often release a heavy dose of
acids. The meltwater in swamps and temporary forest pools may
be too acidic for frogs and other amphibians to reproduce.

In the wintertime, snow usually remains frozen on the land, its acids stored on the outside of ice particles. The first thaw releases most of these concentrated pollutants. Norwegian scientists found that the first 30 percent of meltwater from snow and ice releases 50 to 80 percent of the acids. Since acid-laden snow may collect for many weeks, a strong dose of acids can be released in one late winter or spring thaw.

One example of this pulse of acidity, as scientists call it, was observed at the Adirondack's Panther Lake. The lake's normal pH is about 7. In the spring of 1979, however, its pH dropped temporarily to about 5—a hundred times more acidic.

Panther Lake had enough acid neutralizing capacity to rebound from such an acid pulse, but many lakes do not. A sharp increase in acidity can kill fish. In 1975 thousands of trout died in Norway's Tovdal River as a result of a thaw that freed stored acids from snow. Some scientists believe that such acid jolts, rather than a gradual drop in pH, may be responsible for most of the harm to aquatic life, especially in streams.

Through field observations and laboratory experiments, biologists have learned a lot about how increasing acidity affects life in freshwater lakes and streams. More than fish die. Acid rain causes the death of water-inhabiting insects and other creatures that fish eat, and eventually the demise of an entire ecosystem, except for those organisms that thrive under highly acidic conditions.

Below is a "diary of death" that describes some of the effects on aquatic life as their surroundings become more acidic. It is adapted in part from Thomas Pawlick's book, *A Killing Rain,* which is listed in the Further Reading section at the back of this book.

At pH 6.5, the growth rate of brook trout slows and lake trout begin to have trouble reproducing. Clams and snails become scarce. Acid-tolerant organisms, such as certain rotifers and filamentous green algae, start to increase.

At pH 6, brook and rainbow trout populations start to decline. Smallmouth bass and spotted salamanders have trouble reproducing, as do several kinds of mayflies. Several species of clams and snails are wiped out.

At pH 5.8, tiny crustaceans called copepods die out, and some kinds of crayfish have trouble regrowing their hard exoskeletons after they molt.

At pH 5.5, rainbow trout and some smallmouth bass populations become extinct. Other trout, shiners, walleyed pike, and roach fail to reproduce and their numbers drop. Leeches and mayfly larvae disappear.

At pH 5.4, the reproduction of most crayfish is impaired.

At pH 5, all but one species of crayfish are dead, as are brook trout, walleyed pike, and bullfrogs. Thick mats of green and blue-green algae cover the lake bottom. Some insects increase because few fish are left to prey on them or because they live on the water surface. These include water boatmen and water striders.

At pH 4.8, the numbers of leopard frogs decline, along with populations of rooted underwater pond weeds.

At pH 4.5, mayflies and stoneflies have all died out.

At pH 4.3, pumpkinseed sunfish populations decline and northern pike have disappeared.

At pH 4.2, the common toad dies out. It lives on land but must lay its eggs in ponds and lakes.

At pH 4, the spring peeper, another amphibian that reproduces in ponds and marshes, begins to die out. All aquatic plants except those that are acid tolerant are dead or in decline.

At pH 3.5, virtually all clams, snails, frogs, fish, and crayfish are missing from these highly acidic waters.

At pH 2.5, only a few species of acid-tolerant midges and some algae and fungi are alive.

At pH 2, the water is remarkably clear, but this is not a healthy clarity. The water is virtually sterile.

As lakes grow more acidic, crayfish first fail to grow normal exoskeletons, then fail to reproduce, and die out.

Many of these grim details were established in a re-
markable eight-year study at a Canadian lake that scientists deliberately made more acidic. In 1969 the
Canadian government established the Experimental
Lakes Area in northwestern Ontario. Forty-six lakes in
the area were to be used for tests on the effects of pollution, or as undisturbed controls with which the experimental lakes could be compared. The lakes are
similar to thousands of others in eastern Canada, un-
derlain with granite and low in acid neutralizing capacity. However, they lie in a region where prevailing winds
do not bring much acid precipitation.

In 1974 a nameless lake, given the number 223, was
chosen for study of the effects of acidification. Lake 223
is 68 acres in area with a maximum depth of 47 feet. A
team of scientists from the Freshwater Institute of Winnipeg, led by Dr. David Schindler, studied the lake and
its life under normal conditions during 1974 and 1975.
Its pH was then 6.8. In 1976 they began adding sulfuric
acid, spilling it slowly into the propeller wash of a boat
that crisscrossed the lake several times over a period of
one to two hours. This was done each May, with just
enough acid put in the water to reach a target pH set
for that year. Acid was added throughout the ice-free
season to keep the pH near, but not below, the target
value the scientists had set.

Some of the specific effects the scientists observed are
included in the "diary of death" on the previous pages.
As pH dropped to near 6 in the first two years, the slight
changes in plant and animal populations were in the
normal range for lakes in the area of lake 223. In 1978,
however, the biologists found that several key organisms

in the lake's food web were severely affected when the average pH dropped to 5.93. An abundant crustacean, the opossum shrimp, practically disappeared. The fathead minnow, a small fish that was food for trout, failed to reproduce.

In 1980, with the average lake pH at 5.59, the biologists found that fathead minnows were scarce. Another minnow species, the pearl dace, was more acid tolerant and increased rapidly with its competition gone. Crayfish failed to reproduce. Although biologists had seen lake trout spawn in the fall of 1978, they found no young trout in 1980. Similarly, in the spring of 1981 they saw suckers spawning but observed no young suckers that summer.

The numbers of trout and suckers over one year of age remained high. These adult fish continued to grow at a rate similar to fish in nearby normal lakes. If a fisherman had come upon lake 223 in the summer of 1981, he would have found large and plentiful adult fish. The fishing might have been exceptionally good; with many food species of trout in decline, hungry trout might have been easily attracted to lures or bait. But no young fish were being reproduced and the food web that supported the older fish was disintegrating.

The big trout gave a false impression of the lake's health. This led the biologists to warn other scientists that most kinds of large fish are *not* sensitive indicators of the early stages of damage caused by increasing acidity.

In 1982 the usual breeding sites of lake trout were covered with growths of algae. The trout spawned in new sites, but no young trout hatched from the eggs.

In 1979 the lake trout of lake 223 still had abundant food and appeared normal (above). In 1982, with the lake's pH at 5.1, the adult trout were emaciated (below), and no young were being produced.

By the autumn of 1983, with the pH of lake 223 near 5, no fish of any kind had reproduced successfully. Increasingly, trout were being eaten by other trout because minnows, crayfish, and other natural foods were so scarce. The trout had also become skinny, misshapen creatures.

In a report of lake 223's acidification, published in the journal *Science*, David Schindler and his colleagues wrote that some of the adverse changes occurred much earlier than they had expected. Also, some of the effects they discovered were so subtle or complex that they would have been undetected in a small-scale study or in a laboratory.

They found, for example, that crayfish were harmed in several ways by the increasing acidity of lake 223. These crustaceans were unable to produce enough calcium for their exoskeletons. They also suffered from increased infestations of parasites, and perhaps from increased predation by trout. In addition, fewer crayfish eggs and young survived. All of these stresses in their lake environment helped finish off the crayfish.

Acid rain has other indirect effects on aquatic life. In New York's Adirondack Mountains, biologist Carl Schofield of Cornell University has studied the decline and disappearance of fish from many lakes. He found that some losses occurred at pH levels that were not usually considered lethal to fish and concluded that some other factor must be at work. He guessed it was aluminum.

Acids cause aluminum and other metals to be released from soils and lake sediments. Other metals freed by acids include lead, mercury, cadmium, zinc, and nickel. In some areas metals become so concentrated in the tissues of fish and other animals that they may pose a health threat to humans. In Sweden, for example, moose browsing on plants in acidified lakes have so much cadmium in their livers that the government has warned hunters not to eat moose liver. Near acidified lakes in Canada, raccoons have five times the normal amount of mercury in their livers.

Aluminum, the third most abundant element in the earth's crust, is plentiful in most soils. Normally it is bound to other molecules, but acids break these chemical bonds. In some areas of North America and northern Europe, acid rain releases so much aluminum that it can be seen glistening on the surfaces of lakes in the springtime.

In the case of trout, as Carl Schofield suggested, research showed that aluminum can damage the gills of fish enough to kill them. It coats the gills and causes mucus to form, which interferes with a fish's intake of vital nutrients and of oxygen. The fish may literally suffocate. Laboratory studies confirm that aluminum harms fish, even in waters with a pH as high as 5.9, a level of acidity that many fish can normally tolerate.

Laboratory research has also shown that increased acidity affects the internal chemistry of freshwater fish. Like all living animals, they must keep a certain chemical balance in their body fluids. Fish must take in and retain sodium in order to keep the salinity (saltiness) of their fluids at proper levels. When the acid content of water increases, there is more hydrogen but less sodium available to fish. As they absorb the available elements from the water, the acidity of their blood rises and the salinity drops. This kills brown trout at a pH of 5.2.

Fish and other organisms differ in their sensitivity to acidity. Brown trout are able to survive in more acidic water than lake trout. One variety of brook trout in Canada seemed somewhat resistant to acidity. In a New York fish hatchery this hardy trout was crossbred with local varieties in an attempt to produce fish that would survive in Adirondack lakes where native brook trout had already disappeared. The offspring, however, survived as poorly as native trout.

Amphibians are among the most acid-sensitive of all aquatic organisms. Many frogs, toads, and salamanders breed in small ponds or temporary forest pools, not in large lakes. These shallow waters may become highly acidic as they fill with meltwater from snow in the spring. Canadian biologist Karen Clark reported the pH values of twelve ponds in the spring: eight were below pH 5, some as low as 4.5. The lower the pH, the lower the hatching success of amphibian eggs.

Laboratory studies have shown that acidity affects an enzyme that makes hatching possible. Karen Clark reported another effect:

"There also appears to be a toughening or failure to expand of the membrane around the embryo, so that the embryo when it is ready to hatch can't get out. Normally they would wiggle until they break through, but in the eggs from the acid environment the embryos were unable to get out. . . . Those that did finally get out had deformed spines.

"The presence of aluminum seems to enhance the effect. And then there is something else that happens. At low pH the eggs take longer to hatch,

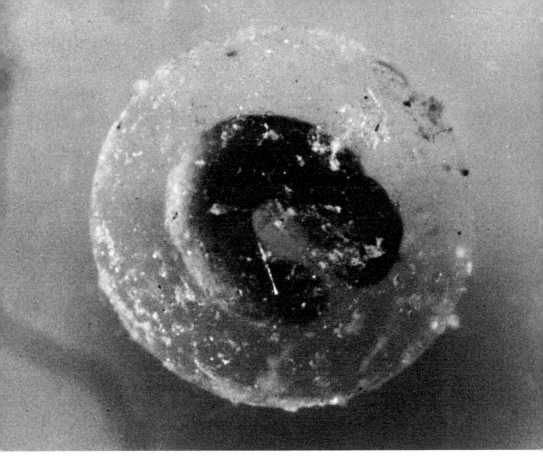

The spring peeper embryo shown above developed normally in water of pH 7.

sometimes three or four days longer, and during the delay a fungus often infects the eggs. The growth of the fungus seems to be encouraged by acidity, and the delay in hatching gives it more time to envelop the eggs. The embryos eventually hatch, breaking through the egg membrane, but the long filaments of fungus are there, and they can't get out of the fungus. So they die anyway."

Acid deposition has stilled the voices of countless wood frogs, spring peepers, and American toads, re-

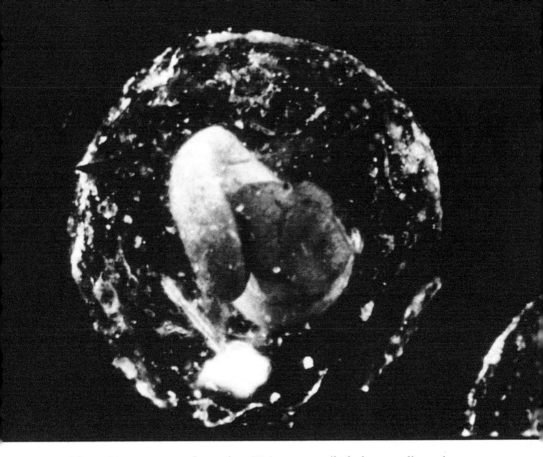

This spring peeper embryo, in pH 4 water, coiled abnormally and failed to hatch.

ducing populations of these and other amphibians that are little noticed but important members of forest ecosystems. Acid rain also affects other creatures that spend part of their lives in or near ponds, lakes, and streams. Otters, herons, mergansers, and loons all eat fish, crayfish, and other aquatic animals. They find little or no food in hundreds of highly acidic lakes. According to biologists in the province of Quebec, mergansers and kingfishers are seen only on lakes that have pH values above 5.6.

Loon populations are dwindling in some areas as a

result of acid rain. Canadian biologist Robert Alvo learned something about the decline of these magnificent diving birds by observing them on lakes near Sudbury, Ontario. Some lakes in the region are among the most acidic in North America, with pH levels as low as 4. Other lakes have enough acid neutralizing capacity in their basins to remain healthy. In the summer of 1982, Robert Alvo surveyed eighty-four lakes and found that healthy lakes had more successful breeding loon pairs than did acidic lakes. To his surprise, however, he discovered that loons continued to nest and successfully hatch young on acidic lakes. Then something happened to the young loons after they hatched. Alvo found that only 14 percent of young loons died on healthy lakes, but 62 percent died on acidic lakes.

The young loons died during a period, about eleven weeks long, when they could not fly and had to rely on their home lake for food. Robert Alvo wondered whether the young loons were starving to death. Through a telescope he observed loon families on both healthy and somewhat acidic lakes. He found that "During the first month of life, chicks were fed very small food items and small fish; but later they were fed mostly fish. During the latter stage, the parents on the somewhat acidified lakes had to dive more frequently than the parents on the healthy lakes to capture the same number of fish."

In 1985 he watched a loon family on Majorie Lake, where loon chicks had failed to mature for at least three summers in a row. Majorie Lake is 185 acres in size, dotted with several small islands, and a beautiful sight. But it is highly acidic, fishless, and probably also completely barren of crayfish, frogs, and most aquatic insects. Dense mats of algae cover its bottom.

Robert Alvo watched the parent loons try to feed their lone chick. Almost every time they dove they came up with something for the little bird. Sadly, it wasn't fish. It appeared to be algae, which possibly held small insects if any survived in the lake. When the chick foraged for itself near shore, it seemed to be catching whirligig beetles, which were abundant there. These insects live on the water surface and therefore are able to survive on acidic lakes.

The parent loons did not seem to seek food for themselves in Majorie Lake but took turns flying off to fish in a healthy lake. Unlike some other bird species, however, the common loon does not bring food from afar to its young. So the loon chick was entirely dependent

Acidic lakes become death traps for young loons, which cannot develop normally on the little food that survives in the water.

on what Majorie Lake had to offer and probably died before its wing feathers grew and it could fly away.

Robert Alvo concluded, "Even if the loons return during the next few years, they will have no chance of breeding success."

In 1987 biologists in Canada and the United States announced the results of studies that tied acid rain to a sharp decline of black ducks. Populations of this duck, a major waterfowl species, have dropped by 60 percent since 1955. Its breeding range coincides closely with regions of acid-sensitive lakes, especially in Canada.

Biologists of the United States Fish and Wildlife Service raised black ducklings on experimental ponds with high and low levels of acidity. They found that three times as many ducklings died on the acidic ponds. Observations in the wild by the Canadian Wildlife Service showed that young black ducks in moderately acidic areas grew at a rate 60 percent slower than those in nonacidic areas. Many of the young ducks starved to death, apparently because acidity had reduced the abundance and diversity of food available in lakes and ponds. A Canadian biologist said, "We now know that acid-stressed lakes do not produce many baby ducks."

Acid rain is most deadly in lakes and ponds, whose basins collect acids, metals, and any other pollutants that seep downhill in watersheds. It also harms life in rivers and streams, even though flowing waters are continually replenished. Strong pulses of acidity from spring snowmelt are especially deadly to stream life.

Several Nova Scotia salmon rivers no longer sustain spawning runs of these great fish. In the early 1980s eight rivers had annual pH values below 4.7. Their salmon runs were extinct. According to Dr. Walton Watt of Canada's Department of Fisheries and Oceans, "For several of these rivers there are angling records going back over a hundred years which show fairly steady catches until the 1950s, when a decline set in, and in most cases no angling catch by 1970. An electrofishing survey in the summer of 1980 failed to show any sign of Atlantic salmon reproduction."

Thirteen other Nova Scotia rivers had pH measurements in the range of 4.7 to 5, and their salmon runs were declining. Nine other rivers had a pH range of 5.1 to 5.4, considered unhealthy for salmon survival. Walton Watt predicted the extinction of salmon runs in at least eleven more rivers by the end of the century unless the rate of acidification was reduced.

Salmon have also declined in rivers that are moderately acidic, both in Nova Scotia and New England. Acid itself may interfere with the ability of the fish to find their home streams for spawning. Odors are the clues that enable salmon to find their way home to spawn at their own place of birth. In a laboratory experiment at the University of New Hampshire, salmon exposed to acid waters became indifferent to odors that normally attracted them, and swam toward odors they would normally ignore. Acids in the water either changed the molecules of odors or the way the fish perceived them.

These laboratory observations were supported by reports from Sweden, where biologists have seen salmon reach the mouths of their home rivers, yet fail to swim upstream. Marked salmon have also been found spawning in places that were not their birthplace, even though their home spawning area was accessible. Acids in the water may be leading the fish astray, perhaps to low-quality spawning sites. This effect occurs at pH in the range of 5 to 6, which usually is not low enough to harm salmon eggs or young. The acidity may still jeopardize salmon reproduction, however, by changing the behavior of the fish.

Acid deposition may also interfere in the reproduction of other fish that are commonly thought to be ocean dwellers. Many of the striped bass that range along the East Coast are born in the freshwater tributaries of Chesapeake Bay. About 150 rivers and smaller streams carry water into the vast bay. They also carry acids and such metals as aluminum that acids have freed from soils. Parts of the bay's watershed have sufficient acid neutralizing capacity, but large areas along both its eastern and western shores do not.

Experiments have shown that newly hatched bass, just a few days old, are killed by acid waters, especially when aluminum is also present. Young fish suffered an extremely high death rate when put in water from one Chesapeake Bay tributary, the Nanticoke River, which is one of the bay's most important spawning streams. The water contained high concentrations of aluminum, and its pH was 6.3. The optimum pH for young striped bass is 7.5; they usually die in water of pH 6.5 or less.

Striped bass have reproduced poorly in Chesapeake Bay since the early 1970s. Their population has dropped sharply. These fish have long been a favorite seafood for many people. Now they are seldom available because commercial catches have dropped 90 percent, and some states have banned catching the fish altogether in an effort to help the species survive. No one blames acid rain alone for this decline, but some biologists believe that only a reduction in acid rain will enable striped bass to recover.

Public concern and scientific attention has been focused on the waters that are made more acidic by acid deposition. Nevertheless, acids fall on all sorts of environments, and in some places cause lakes to become *more alkaline*. This phenomenon was first reported in 1982 by Peter Kilham of the Division of Biological Sciences at the University of Michigan.

Kilham studied Weber Lake, which lies in the northern part of lower Michigan in a region whose carbonate bedrock provides strong acid neutralizing capacity. He compared the lake's chemistry with measurements taken in the 1950s and found that its alkalinity had doubled in thirty years. By 1982 the lake's pH had climbed to a range of 7.2 to 8.2. Sulfur compounds entering the lake are neutralized by bacteria in soils and sediments; nitrogen compounds are taken up by plants. Before being neutralized, however, the acidic compounds release carbonates from rocks in the lake's watershed, adding to the water's alkalinity.

Life in the lake changed as its pH rose. Algae and microorganisms that used to thrive in the slightly acidic water of Weber Lake disappeared. They were replaced by species commonly found in alkaline water. Weber Lake also became more eutrophic—rich in nutrients and minerals. Nutrient-rich lakes are highly productive of life but eventually become oxygen poor, choked with decaying algae and other vegetation. This process is called eutrophication.

Summing up his report on Weber Lake, Peter Kilham

wrote, "Acidification kills fish while alkalization makes lakes more eutrophic. Unfortunately, neither is a desirable result."

People associate acid rain with proven damage to waters in eastern North America, but parts of the West are potentially more vulnerable. Many lakes in the Sierra Nevada, Colorado Rockies, and Washington Cascades have low acid neutralizing capacities. Western mountains also have steeper slopes and thinner soils than those in the East, so acid deposition may reach lakes and streams more quickly, with little chance of being neutralized. The large volumes of snow could yield strong acid doses during spring melt.

In the mid-1980s there was little evidence that existing levels of acid deposition in the West had caused harm, but few scientists had looked for such damage. "My

Much of the mountainous West has low acid neutralizing capacity and will be harmed if acid deposition increases.

guess is that damage will occur," said John Harte, a University of California biologist. "The question is, do we have 80 years before biological damage occurs, or are we talking about ten years?"

In eastern North America there was no doubt about the toll taken by acid deposition. The province of Ontario counted 220 lakes that were too acid to support much life. Nearly 4,000 other lakes were becoming steadily more acidified, with more than 40,000 lakes threatened if acid precipitation was not reduced.

In the Adirondack Mountains of New York, more than half of all lakes above 2,000 feet in elevation had pH values of less than 5. No fish survived in nine out of ten of these lakes. Several hundred others were judged to be in danger of losing their fish.

State after state reported a mounting toll. Brook trout failed to reproduce in all of the Maine lakes sampled that were located above 2,000 feet in elevation. On Cape Cod eight of the ten best fishing ponds were too acidic to support trout. The state of Pennsylvania stood to lose more than 5,000 miles of prime trout streams to acidification. Aquatic life was also threatened in the Great Smoky Mountain National Park of North Carolina and Tennessee. Some lakes in Florida's sandy central highlands have pH readings below 5, and populations of skinny, stunted bass.

The tally could go on, but the facts tend to lose impact and become meaningless statistics. They may become more real if you imagine yourself on the shore of a lake in Ontario, in the Adirondacks, or in a similar place. Perhaps you have a vacation home or a campsite that you and your family have visited for many years. You

Once the process of acidification is reversed, brook trout and other lake life can be restored.

have memories and old photos of fat trout caught in the lake. You can close your eyes and remember the rhythmic calls of frogs in the spring and the ghostly wails of loons in the summer.

Then imagine how the slow poison of acid rain stills the loons and frogs. Few swallows or kingfishers visit— there are no longer enough insects or fish to catch. Your lake is still beautiful, but its beauty is all surface, like cosmetics on a corpse. Not quite a corpse, because thick mats of acid-tolerant algae grow luxuriantly underwater. But your lake is no longer a lively, complex ecosystem that attracts wildlife from afar.

Many thousands of people have had this experience and, sad to say, many more will probably suffer this loss. One Adirondack resident said, "It is like watching a good friend die."

For all of those who care about the loss of such lakes, ponds, and streams, there is hope: The process of acidification is not irreversible; its harmful effects are not permanent. When acid deposition is reduced enough, the natural processes that produce acid neutralizing compounds will gradually raise pH readings of most and perhaps all lakes and streams.

Research at Hubbard Brook Experimental Forest by Gene Likens showed that the life of a stream can rebound quickly once acids decrease. Other findings that support this hope for lakes were published in the journal *Science* in May 1986. David Schindler and his co-workers had studied the water chemistry of another lake—number 239—in the Experimental Lakes Area in northwestern Ontario. The region has low acid neutralizing capacity, but the scientists noticed that the water within the lakes often had higher alkalinity values than the water of their inflowing streams. This suggested that processes within the lakes were effective acid neutralizers.

For three years the scientists studied lake 239, collecting data on the chemical composition of precipitation, of water flowing into the lake, and of water flowing

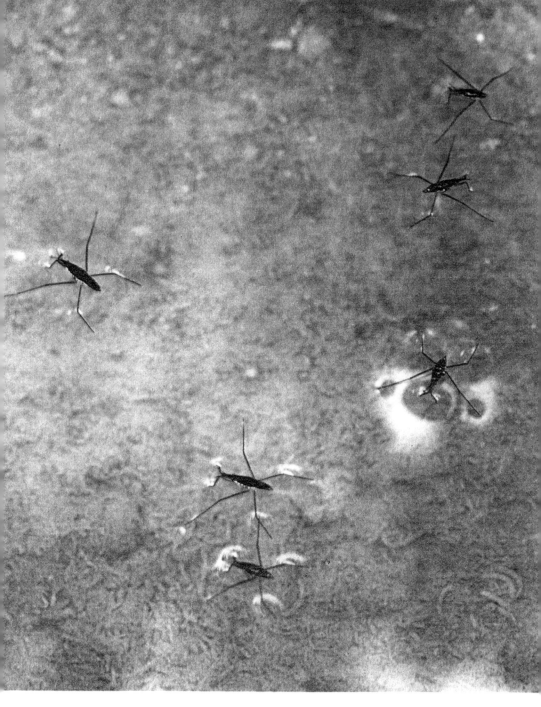

Hundreds of lakes now support only acid-tolerant algae and such surface-dwelling insects as water striders. Restoring the normal complex ecosystems of these lakes will not be easy.

out. From these data they established an "alkalinity budget" and discovered that a great deal of lake 239's alkalinity was produced by the process of respiration in underwater plants and of decay in sediments. Their report concluded, "We predict that the recovery of alkalinity to normal values in lakes should be relatively rapid once the acidity of atmospheric deposition is reduced."

Each lake has a unique alkalinity budget, and some will recover more slowly than others. The most acidic lakes may take decades to return to their natural water chemistry. Then people will have the challenge of restoring, as best they can, the complex ecosystems wrecked by acid deposition. It won't be just a matter of stocking trout or bass, but of reestablishing populations of crayfish, minnows, frogs, insects, plants, and microorganisms.

Many people who have witnessed the decline of a favorite pond or lake may not live long enough to see its ecological restoration. Once acid deposition is sharply reduced, however, their children and grandchildren may experience this rebirth.

4

Forest Decline and Damaged Lungs

The harmful effects of acid rain do not stop at the water's edge, but studying and understanding these effects on living trees or on soil microorganisms is extremely difficult. The available evidence suggests, however, that acid deposition, along with other air pollutants, damages forests and human health. Acid rain also inflicts several billion dollars of damage each year on buildings and other structures.

Some scientists believe that acid rain plays a major role in the widespread decline of forests in Europe and in high-altitude regions of eastern North America. In West Germany this plague is called *waldsterben*—forest death. It was first noticed in the early 1970s, when white fir trees began to die out. Eventually other species were affected. In 1982 some trees in 8 percent of all forests in West Germany seemed to be in poor health. In 1985 the area in which some trees showed visible symptoms of decline increased to an estimated 52 percent. (Few trees died as a result of this decline, because German foresters cut trees as soon as they become unhealthy.)

Damage has also been reported in twelve other European nations. Forest death affects four of the most important coniferous species and seven broad-leaved

---

The crown of a silver fir in the Black Forest shows symptoms of what German foresters call forest death.

species in Europe, including beech, silver birch, ash, and two kinds of oak.

West Germany's Black Forest and Bavarian Forest have been especially hard-hit by *waldsterben*. Trees have stunted, deformed root systems and other abnormal growth symptoms. Some have lost more than half of their foliage. In their weakened condition they are vulnerable to damage by insects, fungi, and wind. Some plants on the forest floor area are also dying. In some cases the underground fungi called mycorrhizae are missing or scarce. These fungi are vital to the well-being of many plants, as they aid in the uptake of water and nutrients from the soil. Whole forest ecosystems are changing.

Circumstantial evidence suggests that acid deposition contributes to this forest death. Brown coal with high sulfur content is burned as fuel in Eastern Europe, and rainfall with an average pH of 3.8 falls on mountainous forests along Czechoslovakia's borders with Poland and East Germany. Damage to trees is severe in this region.

Bernard Ulrich of West Germany's Göttingen University has studied beech and spruce trees whose crowns have died. A tree's crown is where new growth normally occurs. Ulrich discovered that fine tree roots are damaged when calcium is depleted from the soil and aluminum is present in high concentrations. When its fine roots are damaged, a tree grows more slowly, is less able to take up water and nutrients, and is less resistant to disease. Since acid rain frees aluminum in soils, it is a prime suspect in the cause of crown death in beech and spruce trees in West Germany.

Forest death is not widespread in North America, but

Many spruce and fir trees have died on Camels Hump and other peaks in the Green Mountains of Vermont.

there are enough signs that a similar process may be under way that scientists in the United States and Canada are concerned. A German scientist familiar with the symptoms of unhealthy spruce trees in Europe examined spruces in Vermont and found the same symptoms. Coniferous trees are dying and failing to reproduce in some eastern high altitude forests. On North Carolina's Mount Mitchell, the highest peak in the East at 6,684 feet, many spruce and fir trees above 5,000 feet have died. On Camels Hump, a high peak in the Green

Mountains of Vermont, more than half of the spruce trees have died since 1965.

Many spruces and firs have died or have dead crowns in the mountains of New Hampshire, in New York's Adirondacks, in Quebec's Laurentians, and in the Appalachians. A forest pathologist in North Carolina reported that high elevation spruce trees in many parts of the southern Appalachians showed signs of decline between 1984 and 1985. And in December 1985 the United States Forest Service reported that the growth of loblolly and slash pine trees in parts of several southern states had slowed during the previous twenty years. In addition to such natural factors as generally drier weather, air pollution may be causing this decline.

Cores that reveal growth rings have been taken from 7,000 living trees in fifteen eastern states. They show that several species have had unusually slow growth for twenty years or more. This symptom went undetected because there were no dramatic outward signs of trouble. It is a warning, however. Research in Europe shows that the forest decline occurring there was also preceded by a largely unnoticed drop in tree growth that began in the 1960s for some species and in the 1970s for others.

In both Europe and North America, the most severely damaged forests grow on high slopes facing prevailing weather systems. Acid rain, ozone, abnormal amounts of nitrogen compounds, and other pollutants may cause this damage, and many scientists are trying to understand exactly how trees and other forest plants are harmed.

On top of Mount Mitchell, forest pathologist Robert Bruck of North Carolina State University said, "There is a vegetable soup of pollutants up here. We have found elevated levels of lead, zinc, and copper in the forest litter [dead leaves and other organic debris on the ground], and seven days out of ten the mountain is bathed in cloud moisture that is often one hundred times more acidic than normal rainfall."

Bruck added, however, "I can't say with any confidence . . . that air pollution is killing these trees. We hope to find out. But it appears that whatever is happening is so complex that it could take a long time."

Laboratory research at the University of Vermont showed that exposure to either acid rain or certain met-

---

Forest researchers are trying to understand the effects of acid rain—and of aluminum it frees in soils—on the roots of trees.

als stunted the growth of trees, mosses, fungi, and algae. When plants were given both acidified water and small amounts of aluminum, zinc, or other metals, their growth slowed abruptly and some died.

University of Vermont scientists also made chemical analyses of tree growth cores that had been collected all through the twentieth century. Hubert Vogelmann, chairman of the university's botany department, reported, "Preliminary core samples indicate that the content of aluminum in the wood changed very little from the early 1900s until about 1950. At that time, the period associated with the beginnings of acid rain, the concentration of aluminum increased dramatically and in some samples was three times higher than before."

Thus research in both Vermont and in West Germany suggests that acid rain's ability to free the common element aluminum in the soil may be among the factors causing forest decline. However, scientists know that other air pollutants also harm trees. Ozone gas, which forms when nitrogen oxides and hydrocarbons react with oxygen in the air, causes leaf cells to rupture. Excessive amounts of nitrogen compounds also may be responsible for some damage to forests. In addition to nitrogen oxides from power plants and automobiles, ammonia and other nitrogen compounds enter the atmosphere from heavily fertilized fields.

The nitrogen and sulfur in acid deposition actually fertilize some trees and other plants growing in nutrient-poor soils. This has been observed in Sweden and Norway, where growth rates of pines and spruces increased in some areas. Scandinavian scientists warned, however, that this positive effect would eventually end, probably with a sharp drop in growth, as a result of the loss of other nutrients from soils, caused by acidic compounds. In 1985 Swedish scientist Bengt Nihlgård said, "Excess nitrogen may make the trees more productive in the beginning, but also more sensitive to other air pollutants, frost, and biological enemies."

Hubert Vogelmann suspected that nitrogen was the source of trouble in the winter of 1983–1984, when thousands of red spruce and other trees in Vermont suffered unusual frost damage. The trees did not seem to have their normal resistance to frost. One theory is that excess nitrogen causes plant cells to keep growing late in the year and leaves them unable to withstand severe winter weather.

Many scientists in Europe and North America believe that a combination of air pollutants, including acid rain, puts forests under great stress. Hubert Vogelmann said, "These forests are being hammered by all of them. It's pretty hard to isolate one and suggest that it is more of a cause than all of the rest."

There is a range of opinion among scientists about the causes of forest decline. Some of those working for federal agencies have been extremely reluctant to implicate acid rain. A United States Forest Service scientist said, "Insects, drought, management practices, and many other factors influence forests. It is awfully early to blame air pollution alone, although the long-range transport of pollutants has been proved. We need between three and ten years of further research to understand what's occurring."

In 1987 University of Vermont botanist Richard Klein agreed on the need for research but also said, "Modern

Acid deposition may contribute to the decline of sugar maple trees, and of maple syrup production.

forest decline in North America, Europe, and parts of East Asia is unquestioned. It is not due to insects, disease, or drought, although these factors add to other stresses on forests. The causes are extremely complex, involving four or five major human-caused pollutants, some affecting leaves, some roots. More tree species are becoming involved, and symptoms are beginning to show up in the western United States and British Columbia."

Although high-altitude evergreen species were affected first, such broad-leaved trees as beech and maple are also in trouble in the Northeast. Sugar maples over much of the Northeast are in decline. This is especially troubling in Vermont, the nation's leading producer of maple syrup. (Some consumers believe that *all* maple syrup comes from Vermont, but it is produced in many northern states and in Canada.)

Quebec seems to be the maple-syrup-producing area hardest hit by sugar maple decline. A 1982 survey found that 32 percent of the trees in sugar bushes (woods in which sugar maples predominate) were dead or had lost many leaves. A more extensive survey in 1986 found 82 percent of the trees in decline. Dozens of maple syrup producers in Quebec have gone out of business. In 1985 losses in the Canadian maple syrup industry were estimated at $87.6 million. There has been little research on the decline of sugar maples, but scientists expect that pollutants, including the acids that rain down on the Northeast, are the likely cause.

Acid deposition may also do long-term damage to the complex world of living and nonliving things that make up soils of forests and farms. This is under investigation by agricultural scientists. Acid deposition may have some beneficial effects on some farm soils, but most farmers must add lime to the land in order to neutralize acids. According to calculations of the Swedish Ministry of Agriculture, of the lime applied to farmland there, between 5 and 15 percent "is needed to keep acid deposition in check."

Spokesmen for electric utilities and others opposed to controls on acid rain have argued that the acids are vital for agriculture. Concerning the idea of acid rain as fertilizer, Dr. Norman Glass of the Environmental Protection Agency said, "The notion that it is essential or desirable, or even marginally acceptable to continue

supplying sulfur indiscriminately by using polluted
masses of air instead of controlled applications of fertilizer is just that—fertilizer."

In laboratory experiments, artificial acid rain has actually increased the yield of some food plants. It has
damaged the leaves of many vegetable crops, but the
injury occurs at pH levels that are lower than normally
experienced outdoors. The EPA's 1983 report *The Acidic
Deposition Phenomenon and Its Effects* stated that acid rain
leached calcium and other vital nutrients from the leaves
of bean seedlings at pH 4 or less. Actual tissue damage
to leaves occurred at pH 3. In the northeastern United
States, some rainfalls measure 3.5 or less on the pH scale
but the average is about 4.

An experiment on soybeans showed that acid rain

In a laboratory, simulated rain of pH 2.6 injured these radish
leaves, but rainfall is not that acidic.

caused a reduction in seed yield, even when fertilizers and lime were added to the soil. Soybeans exposed to simulated rain of pH 4.1, 3.3, and 2.7 were, respectively, 10.7, 16.8, and 22.9 percent less productive than plants exposed to rain of pH 5.6. This suggested that soybeans, an important livestock food and export crop, may suffer growth losses from the average acidity of Northeast rainfall.

A reduction of just 1 percent in soybean yields would cost farmers in eleven eastern states an estimated $53 million annually. Proving the existence of such a loss is difficult, however, given the year-to-year variations in crop yields that are caused by changes in weather and many other factors. Even if soybeans or other crops suffered losses of several percent each year from acid deposition, the harm might go undetected.

Overall, however, in the mid-1980s agricultural scientists had found no clear evidence that acid rain harmed farm crops significantly. The available evidence suggested that ozone and sulfur dioxide (the precursor of acid sulfate) were more harmful to food plants than acid deposition.

It is well established that acids leach such metals as aluminum, lead, and cadmium from the soil. In addition to entering bodies of water and living plants, these metals reach groundwater that may be tapped for human consumption. Acids in the water can also corrode lead and copper directly from water pipes, and lead and cadmium from the solder that is used to seal joints in nonlead pipes.

A 1979 investigation by the New York State Department of Health sampled water from thirty communities

As the waters of Quabbin Reservoir became more acidic, more lead was eroded from pipes; unsafe concentrations of lead were found in Boston's tap water. Now the water is treated to raise its pH.

in the Adirondack Mountains and found that most of the water sources were strongly acidic. In some homes copper pipes were being corroded and the levels of copper in drinking water were above normal. In two cases children had high levels of lead in their blood. Their drinking water, with a pH range of 4.2 to 5.0, flowed through lead pipes. Even when the pipes were well flushed so lead would not accumulate, the water contained four times the federal standard for safe drinking water.

This prompted a 1981 investigation in Canada that also found unusually high levels of lead and copper in the drinking water of cottages in a region hard-hit by acid rain. In one case, the local water was allowed to stand in a cottage's pipes for ten days (not an unlikely situation for a vacation home). During that time the concentration of copper grew to five times the maximum acceptable level, of lead to ten times the safe level. If a person routinely took a quick drink upon arriving at such a cottage, rather than letting the water run for a while, he or she would take in some heavy doses of toxic metals.

This problem has caused many a rural homeowner in Canada, the Adirondacks, and New England to replace lead pipes, and always to let water run a few moments before use. It is more easily solved in large municipal water systems, although at considerable cost. In central Massachusetts, for example, Quabbin Reservoir, which supplies most of Boston's drinking water, has become increasingly acidic. When unsafe levels of lead were found in Boston's water, the Massachusetts Water Resource Authority began adding the alkaline compound sodium hydroxide to raise the pH of Quabbin's water. This reduced the erosion of lead from pipes, but the annual cost ranges from $400,000 to more than $1 million, depending on the fluctuating cost of sodium hydroxide. The state of Massachusetts also changed its plumbing codes, allowing no more lead in solder.

In a more roundabout way, acid rain may threaten human health by increasing the amount of methyl mercury in lake and stream waters, and then in fish that people eat. Methyl mercury accumulates in living tissues and can reach concentrations that harm the human brain, impair vision and hearing, and eventually cause death. It can also cause severe damage to the nervous systems of unborn children in their mother's wombs.

Fish in Scandinavia, eastern Canada, Maine, and New York's Adirondacks have higher than normal concentrations of mercury. The more acidic a lake, researchers have found, the more quickly methyl mercury builds up in the flesh of pike, trout, and other fish. Those with the highest levels of mercury are popular game fish eaten by many people. Individuals who eat a lot of fish caught in acidified lakes are most vulnerable to mercury poisoning. This description fits Cree Indians in Quebec who were, in fact, found to have abnormally high amounts of mercury in their bodies. They also had mild symptoms of mercury poisoning. In both Quebec and Ontario provinces of Canada, people have been warned not to eat fish taken from many lakes and rivers.

Canadian medical researchers also found evidence that linked other human health problems to acid rain. They compared respiratory problems of children living in southern Ontario with those of children living in

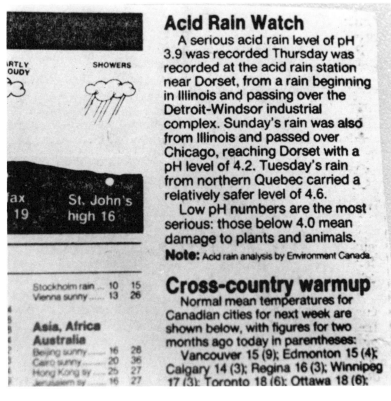

Acid Rain Watch

A serious acid rain level of pH 3.9 was recorded Thursday was recorded at the acid rain station near Dorset, from a rain beginning in Illinois and passing over the Detroit-Windsor industrial complex. Sunday's rain was also from Illinois and passed over Chicago, reaching Dorset with a pH level of 4.2. Tuesday's rain from northern Quebec carried a relatively safer level of 4.6.

Low pH numbers are the most serious: those below 4.0 mean damage to plants and animals.

Note: Acid rain analysis by Environment Canada.

Cross-country warmup

Normal mean temperatures for Canadian cities for next week are shown below, with figures for two months ago today in parentheses:

Vancouver 15 (9); Edmonton 15 (4); Calgary 14 (3); Regina 16 (3); Winnipeg 17 (3); Toronto 18 (6); Ottawa 18 (6);

(partial weather panel) PARTLY CLOUDY · SHOWERS · max 19 · St. John's high 16

Stockholm rain ... 10 15
Vienna sunny 13 26

Asia, Africa Australia

Beijing sunny 16 28
Cairo sunny 20 36
Hong Kong sy 25 27
Jerusalem sy 16 27

This portion of a weather report in the *Toronto Star* includes a summary of a past week's acid rain. Most Canadians are keenly aware that much of their acid deposition originates in the U.S.

southern Manitoba, which receives much less acid deposition. The Ontario children had a higher incidence of allergies, stuffy noses, and coughs. More children under the age of two were hospitalized with breathing problems, and these hospital admissions increased whenever there were high concentrations of sulfur dioxide, ozone, and sulfates in the air.

It is difficult to distinguish between the harm done by acid deposition or its precursors and that caused by other pollutants. Acid rain's exact toll on human health is unmeasurable, but more and more evidence suggests that there is a toll. Testifying before a Senate subcommittee in 1987, medical doctors from prominent national health groups cited evidence that the same pollutants that lead to acid deposition are a serious threat to human health. The doctors said that the pollutants are an important cause of bronchitis and asthma, especially in children. "The ingredients of acid rain have been shown to adversely affect the respiratory tract and consequently the quality of health of children," testified Dr. Richard Narkewicz, president of the American Academy of Pediatrics.

According to Dr. Thomas Godar, president of the American Lung Association, other people at risk from oxides of nitrogen and sulfur (and ozone) include people over sixty-five; those with asthma, chronic bronchitis, and emphysema; pregnant women; and people with a history of heart disease.

In his testimony, Dr. Philip Landrigan, director of the division of environmental and occupational medicine at the Mount Sinai School of Medicine in New York City, reviewed the evidence from several recently completed studies on the health effects of acid rain. He said, "Acid rain is probably third after active smoking and passive smoking as a cause of lung disease."

The health toll may be unmeasurable, but we can safely conclude that a significant decrease in emissions of acid rain precursors will have beneficial health effects.

 Such a decrease will also lessen the wear and tear on the stone, metal, wood, and other materials of human structures. Some damage is caused by sulfur dioxide, known to increase the corrosion process of metals, and some by sulfuric and nitric acid. The most dramatic impact of acid rain is visible on statues, monuments, bridges, and buildings. In the United States, buildings already harmed by acid rain include Chicago's Field Museum, and the Washington Monument, Lincoln Memorial, and Capitol in Washington, D.C. Chambers beneath the Lincoln Memorial resemble a cave, with stalactites hanging from the ceiling—the result of acids eating away the marble above.

Acid rain changes the surface of marble and limestone

A sandstone figure in Germany's industrial Ruhr area still had distinct features in 1908 (left). By 1969 acidic pollutants had eroded the figure into a faceless hulk (right).

into a crust of gypsum plaster that crumbles or is washed away by precipitation. In sandstone, acid rain causes crystals to form and swell, creating cracks in the stone. Some statues have been so eroded by acids that their facial features are becoming unrecognizable.

Acid rain also attacks painted surfaces of homes and cars. Usually this paint erosion is a slow process, but exceptionally acidic precipitation can visibly scar automobiles. This occurred in 1978 when a local rainfall of pH 2.3 ruined the paint on hundreds of cars in central Pennsylvania. To estimate the overall damage to human structures, the EPA and the Army Corps of Engineers studied conditions in several cities, then applied their findings to 117 metropolitan areas in a seventeen-state area, ranging from Kentucky in the South and Illinois in the Midwest to Maine in the Northeast. Estimated damage by acid rain to buildings and other structures was $5 billion annually.

Loss of visibility is also blamed in part on acid deposition. Sulfate particles scatter light in the atmosphere and reduce visibility. Human-made haze now reduces visibility to an average of eight miles in rural parts of the Northeast, a decrease of up to 40 percent since the early 1950s. In the Ohio River Valley, visibility used to average eight to ten miles; now the average is four miles.

There is no doubt about the major source of these troublesome hazy air masses. Satellite photographs show their paths—from midwestern concentrations of coal-burning power plants, to rural areas in the Northeast that formerly had views of exceptional clarity.

Loss of atmospheric clarity may reduce tourism in some areas. Will people visit a high-peak scenic area in

New England or the Great Smoky Mountains when they know the view may be obliterated by haze? Poor visibility also adds to the difficulty of assuring air safety near airports.

The sulfur and nitrogen that spew out of smokestacks certainly have many harmful effects, great and small. Fortunately, some earlier fears of damage by acid rain have not been realized. Food crops, for example, seem little harmed by acid deposition. But its actual and potential harm to aquatic life, forests, structures, and human health is great.

Our understanding of acid rain and its effects will continue to grow, but the questions that remain have little bearing on the steps needed to control this pollution. In 1986 Gene Likens said, "Unanswered scientific questions represent, at most, 20 percent of the obstacle to action on acid rain control. Economic and political factors have always been the main stumbling block."

5
Remedies

The Edison Electric Institute is a lobbying and public relations organization for the electric utility industry. One of its publications offered a solution for lakes in acid distress: "The most promising strategy for helping lakes with low pH problems is to use lime or limestone to reduce the acidity and raise the pH."

Lake liming has gone on for decades, and scientists know a lot about its effectiveness. Before exploring this chemical treatment in detail, however, an obvious truth should be stated: Adding lime is hardly a promising strategy for helping lakes harmed by acid deposition. As a remedy it is like applying a Band-Aid to the symptoms of a disease. Real solutions attack the disease itself, at its source.

Sweden began adding powdered alkaline compounds to lakes in 1976. Their use doubles or triples the calcium content of the water, and quickly raises the pH from 4 to near 7. The effect lasts for more than ten years if a lake has a slow rate of water replacement, much less if its water is replaced more rapidly.

Running waters are more difficult to treat, and Swedish scientists are experimenting with devices that give streams doses of lime. Called "wet slurry dosers," these devices add fine particles of calcium carbonate to streams, and automatically increase the amount when a rainstorm or melting snow raises the volume of water. They have helped prevent the sharp drops in pH that often kill young fish, and have helped maintain stocks of salmon and trout in some Swedish rivers. Two of these dosers are being used experimentally in the United States on a tributary of Chesapeake Bay to see if this treatment can improve the survival of young striped bass.

Sweden's liming program was begun too late to save fish populations in several thousand lakes. It has been applied where most needed to maintain such valuable species as char, salmon, and crayfish. In general, the addition of calcium compounds has had positive effects on aquatic life, including plankton and crayfish. Mercury levels in pike have dropped. Concentrations of aluminum in lake water also declined, although incoming acidic water from tributaries soon caused aluminum to rise again.

Lake liming is costly, however. From 1976 through 1986 the Swedish government spent $78 million to lime (and sometimes relime) about four thousand lakes. Despite the expense, the National Swedish Environment Protection Board concludes that liming will be necessary as a defense until acidic emissions in Europe are cut.

In North America, liming has helped maintain fish populations in some Cape Cod, Massachusetts, ponds, and has been used experimentally in New York's Adirondack Mountains and in Canada. In the 1970s Canadian scientists carried out liming tests on several acidic lakes near Sudbury, Ontario. Powdered lime and crushed limestone were dumped from boats, and pH

Helicopters drop powdered alkaline compounds into the waters of acidified lakes that cannot easily be reached by vehicles.

levels rose to near 7. Nevertheless, trout died soon after being put in the water. A report of the project concluded, "The liming had failed to reduce the toxic metal concentrations in the sediment, and continued acid rainfall had brought new overdoses, washing in more metals from the land and the sky."

Liming costs about $30 an acre when the cheapest forms of calcium compounds are applied from boats. Some acidic lakes are inaccessible by vehicle, however, and must be limed from the air by helicopters. This boosts the cost to $300 or more an acre. Considering the great number of North American lakes and streams already in need of relief from acid, large-scale lake and stream liming seems prohibitively expensive.

Most aquatic biologists in Canada and the United States take a dim view of this method of treating acid-distressed lakes. Harold Harvey of the University of Toronto said, "Let us dismiss out of hand that we can lime the northeast quadrant of a continent." He added, "If you take an acid lake and lime it, you do not now have a normal lake; you now have a limed, formerly very acid lake, with a very peculiar water chemistry and a very peculiar biota as a result."

Real solutions to the problem of acid deposition cut emissions of the pollutants that cause it. One step is to require more-effective controls on exhausts of autos and other vehicles to reduce emissions of nitrogen oxides. But most nitrogen oxides come from smokestacks, not autos, so the single most important step is to reduce smokestack emissions of both acid rain precursors: nitrogen oxides and sulfur dioxide. In this chapter the ways in which these pollutants can be reduced and some of the pros and cons of each method are described, without venturing deeply into the controversies surrounding these remedies.

Coal is not a uniform substance. Its sulfur content varies, so use of low-sulfur coal is one way to decrease acid deposition. Deposits of high-sulfur coal, which contains more than 3 percent sulfur by weight, are concentrated in northern West Virginia, western Kentucky, Pennsylvania, Indiana, Illinois, and Ohio. Coal burned in these states produces much of the acid that poisons regions to the east.

Low-sulfur coal, containing less than 1 percent sulfur by weight, is mined in several western states and in Virginia, Tennessee, eastern Kentucky, and southern West Virginia. Coal from western states is plentiful and cheap but becomes slightly more costly than midwestern coal when shipped to the Midwest. The chief drawback to large-scale fuel-switching, however, would be the loss of thousands of jobs in the high-sulfur coal-mining industry. This would be a blow to the economy of a region that already has high unemployment. On the other hand, increased use of low-sulfur coal would stimulate employment and business in the regions where that coal is found.

Coal washing also reduces sulfur dioxide emissions, although a lot of high-sulfur coal now burned is already washed. In this process, coal is crushed, passed through filters, and washed so that about half of its pyrite (iron sulfide) is removed. Pyrite contains sulfur. Other sulfur remains chemically bound to the coal and cannot be removed by this method. Coal washing seldom removes more than a quarter of the sulfur present. Nevertheless, wider use of coal washing could cut sulfur dioxide emissions by 10 percent. This process is relatively inexpensive and is a basic part of most proposed acid rain reduction programs.

Any new coal-fired power plant in the United States is required by the EPA to remove from 70 to 90 percent of the sulfur from its smokestack gases, usually by devices called scrubbers. The acid rain problem exists primarily because this rule does not apply to older plants. In 1987 only about 15 percent of coal-burning electric generating plants in the United States used scrubbers.

Technically, scrubbing is called flue-gas desulfurization. It can be a wet or dry process. In the more common wet process, hot smoky gases from the power plant's coal fire rise up a huge metal cylinder and pass through jets of water containing fine bits of limestone. The lime and sulfur react to form liquid calcium sulfite. Some of it quickly reacts with oxygen to form calcium sulfate. As the hot gases rise out of the plant's smokestacks with 90 percent or more of the sulfur removed, the wet wastes fall to the bottom of the scrubber. From there this gray sludge is pumped to a treatment plant where it is mixed with soot and fly ash that also were removed from flue gases. This thickens the sludge and eventually speeds its drying. While the sludge is still half liquid—about the consistency of toothpaste—it is sent by conveyer belt to holding ponds and a landfill area.

This gray muck is produced at the rate of up to 4,000 tons a day in a large power plant. Its blend of 20 percent calcium sulfate and 80 percent calcium sulfite has little value. Calcium sulfate is gypsum, a marketable product that can be made into wallboard, but natural gypsum can be mined at lower cost than gypsum can be recovered from scrubber sludge. Utilities have had little success developing markets for scrubber wastes, so considerable amounts of landfill space must be provided for its disposal.

Scores of employees are required to keep a scrubber operation working, as is up to 3 percent of a power plant's electrical output. Another cost is limestone; scrubbers use about a ton for every ten tons of coal burned. Scrubbers are also expensive to build, particularly when added to an older power plant. From an

The Tennessee Valley Authority's Paradise Fossil Plant, near Drakesboro, Kentucky, has two 600-foot smokestacks and one 800-foot stack. Arrows point to the scrubbers that remove most sulfur from gases that are emitted from two smokestacks. The plant has a dry scrubbing process that each year produces 450,000 tons of marketable gypsum in the form shown below.

environmental point of view, scrubbers have one major flaw, in addition to the huge volumes of waste sludge they produce. They do not reduce nitrogen oxides, the second most important precursor of acid rain east of the Mississippi.

In the 1970s the high cost of oil and of building nuclear power plants led utilities to favor coal as fuel for future electrical generation. Some existing oil-burning power plants were converted to coal as fuel. Most new plants planned for the 1990s and beyond are coal-burners that, as required by law, will have to have the "best system of emission reduction" available. When the law was written, that was scrubbers, but their costs and other drawbacks have stimulated a search for better ways to cut emissions from coal.

Electric utilities and the United States Department of Energy funded research in cleaner coal burning. A 1985 report by the department's Energy Research Advisory Board listed more than a dozen improved ways to burn coal cleanly. The coal industry seems to be on the verge of a fundamental shift to new methods of generating electricity from coal. Unfortunately, however, utilities have found it too costly to convert old plants to these methods. Although they are considering these methods for the future, their old power plants continue to produce acid rain precursors.

One method is called fluidized-bed combustion. Several European power plants already use this technology, as do pilot plants in Kentucky and Colorado. Crushed coal is burned on a bed of limestone through which flow jets of air. Sulfur in the coal reacts with the limestone to form gypsum, which can be sold. The relatively low

temperature of combustion produces few nitrogen oxides, and the whole process is more energy efficient than
conventional coal-burning methods.

Another promising new coal-burning method is called
Limestone Injection Multistage Burner, or LIMB. Limestone is injected into the furnace where crushed coal
burns, and nearly all of the sulfur dioxide is converted
to dry gypsum. In a second combustion zone most of
the nitrogen oxides are removed. The LIMB technology
requires less than a quarter of the space of a scrubber,
is much less expensive, and can be more easily added
to existing power plants.

Perhaps most promising of all is a method called Integrated Gasification Combined Cycle, called IGCC or
just GCC. A pilot IGCC plant began operating in 1984
at Daggett, California. (It is called the Cool Water plant,
not because of the process, but because it was built on
land of the Cool Water ranch.) In this plant, each day
1,000 tons of coal are crushed and mixed with water
and oxygen, then partly burned in a high-temperature,
high-pressure vessel, producing gas. Energy from the
burning gas powers a turbine that produces 65 megawatts of electricity. Before the gas reaches the turbine,
however, a solvent removes nearly all sulfur compounds. These undergo another process that converts
most of them to elemental sulfur, a salable byproduct
worth $100 a ton in 1986. In another cycle, the heat
from the coal-gasification process drives another 55-
megawatt turbine. In all, the plant produces about 120
megawatts of electricity, about 20 of which are needed
to run the plant itself.

The plant routinely removes 95 to 99 percent of sulfur

Trainloads of coal with varying amounts of sulfur have been tested at the Cool Water plant in California. Its Integrated Gasification Combined Cycle process is shown in the diagram below and described in the text at left.

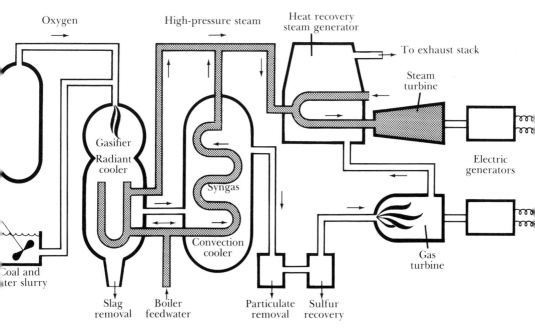

Oxygen

High-pressure steam

Heat recovery
steam generator

To exhaust stack

Steam
turbine

Gasifier

Radiant
cooler

Electric
generators

Syngas

Convection
cooler

Gas
turbine

Coal and
water slurry

Slag
removal

Boiler
feedwater

Particulate
removal

Sulfur
recovery

from coal. Among the coals tested has been a high-sulfur type (3.5 percent sulfur) from Illinois. For each megawatt of electricity generated, the IGCC plant emits from .14 to 4 tons of sulfur dioxide a year. In contrast, a plant with modern scrubbers emits 14 tons of sulfur dioxide per megawatt a year, and a plant without scrubbers emits 140 tons per megawatt a year. The IGCC plant also cuts emissions of nitrogen oxides well below the federal standards for new power plants. Its emission of all pollutants is comparable to, or superior to, those of a power plant burning natural gas, which is the cleanest of fossil fuels.

The pilot IGCC plant at Daggett, California, was built with funds from the Electric Power Research Institute (EPRI) and several companies and utilities, including some from Japan. Dwain Spencer, vice president of advanced power systems at EPRI, said, "We truly believe that we are on the threshold of introducing a *revolutionary* new way of utilizing high-sulfur coal which should be acceptable to the power industry, its customers, regulators, environmentalists, and the general public."

The electric utility industry is enthusiastic about the IGCC technology. While the pilot plant generates 100 megawatts, most new power plants are in the 400- to 600-megawatt range of electrical output. Studies show, however, that full-scale IGCC plants would be quite competitive with either conventional coal-burners or nuclear power plants.

This new technology has another advantage: A utility can add one IGCC unit of about 150-megawatt capacity at a time, rather than build a large conventional power plant. This appeals to most utilities, which have low or uncertain growth of electricity use by their consumers. They have trouble borrowing the money needed for a major 750- to 1,000-megawatt coal or nuclear power plant; even 600 megawatts of new capacity may be excessive. Most utilities would rather add new capacity cautiously, and the IGCC technology may fill their needs. These plants can also be built quickly. The California power plant was constructed in 28 months, while construction of conventional power plants takes twice or three times as long.

In 1987 more than a dozen utilities from coast to coast were investigating IGCC for their needs. Several of these new coal-gasification plants will be complete, producing electricity with little pollution, by 1995. In a report on IGCC and other modern coal-burning methods, Dwain Spencer wrote, "Substitution of new, advanced coal technology as older units are retired appears to be the most sensible approach to achieving meaningful long-term control over air emissions."

In the view of electric utilities, the problem of acid deposition will be solved, perhaps by the year 2020, when all old coal-burning plants have finally been replaced or converted to the new coal-burning processes. The electric power industry is content to wait that long. Environmental groups, Canadian citizens, and most of the general public in the United States are not. They believe that action must be taken soon, even if this means installation of scrubbers, in order to achieve a significant acid rain reduction in this century.

This leads to a scientific question: How much must acid rain precursors be reduced? Several science advi-

Some acidic precipitation falling in Colorado and Idaho appeared to come from copper smelters in Arizona and New Mexico.

sory groups have recommended that the acidity of rain should be reduced by at least half. A 1981 report by the National Academy of Sciences concluded that precipitation with pH values no lower than 4.6 to 4.7 throughout acid-sensitive areas was desirable; that would achieve a reduction of 50 percent in deposited acids.

According to field studies and circumstantial evidence, there is a rough correlation between the amounts of sulfur dioxide that spew from smokestacks and the acids deposited downwind. For example, a sharp increase in sulfur dioxide emissions in the South led to a dramatic increase in acid sulfate deposition, especially in Florida. Temporary declines in emissions, such as those caused by the closing of a copper smelter, have been matched by sharp drops in acid deposition. Therefore, to achieve a 50 percent reduction in acid rain, most scientists recommend a 50 percent reduction in its precursors at their sources.

Utilities have a variety of ways to cut emissions, including their choice of which plants in a system to use the most. To save money, utilities tend to run their most economical plants as much as possible. This often means that scrubber-equipped plants are underused and operate at full capacity only when demand for electricity is greatest. Meeting basic electricity demand with such plants would cost a utility and its customers more, but would also reduce overall emissions from its system.

In the Rocky Mountain states, concern about acid rain has focused on copper smelters. Several smelters in Arizona and New Mexico account for two-thirds of the 1.7 million tons of sulfur dioxide discharged into the air in the region between the Sierras in California and the

Rockies. In the early 1980s, as copper production varied, so did deposits of acid sulfate in the rain and snow that fell as far away as northern Colorado, Idaho, and Wyoming.

One smelter in particular, in Douglas, Arizona, was the largest single uncontrolled source of air pollution in the United States. It had failed to meet deadlines for controls set by the EPA. Spurred on by a lawsuit filed by the Environmental Defense Fund, the EPA insisted that the Douglas smelter cut emissions. It did, dramatically and permanently, by closing for good in January 1987. Another copper smelter in San Manuel, Arizona, continued to operate with largely uncontrolled emissions.

A new copper smelter at Nacozari, Mexico, sixty miles from the Arizona border, began operating without pollution controls in 1986. Under pressure from the United States government, however, Mexico's state copper company hired a Canadian firm to install sulfur dioxide controls by early 1988. Applying this remedy to the Nacozari smelter will spare the West the poison of nearly 500,000 tons of sulfur dioxide a year.

6
The
Politics
of
Acid
Rain

"Death from the Sky" was the headline in the science section of the October 22, 1979, issue of *Newsweek*. Beginning that year, acid rain became a hot subject in magazines, newspapers, and other media. The general public began to be aware of it. According to opinion polls conducted in 1980, about 30 percent of United States citizens surveyed had heard of acid rain. That number more than doubled in the next four years.

Environmental groups called for controls on acid pollutants. The administration of President Jimmy Carter had a record of achievement in environmental protection, but national economic woes and political factors (including hopes for reelection in 1980) made it timid on this issue. In an August 1979 message to Congress, President Carter called acid rain a serious environmental threat of global proportions, but then announced a ten-year research program—the time-honored way of putting off action.

In 1981 President Carter was succeeded by President

The scientific evidence about acid deposition and its effects was used selectively by forces opposed to change and by others who sought to reduce power plant emissions.

Ronald Reagan, who as a candidate had blamed air pollution on trees. The new administration aimed to reduce the size and influence of the federal government, and that goal included removing the threat, or already existing "burden," of environmental regulations on industries.

An early casualty of this approach was the negotiations between the United States and Canada, begun in the Carter administration, that had the goal of establishing a treaty on transboundary air pollution. In 1980 both governments had pledged to work toward such a treaty; scientific and technical groups had been meeting and making progress. The Reagan administration quickly replaced the United States experts and began what seemed to Canadians an attempt to undermine what had already been accomplished.

The attitude that would be held by many in the Reagan administration toward environmental problems was expressed in 1980 by David Stockman as he addressed a business group. (Stockman later became the director of the Office of Management and Budget in the new administration.) On the subject of acid rain he said, "I kept reading these stories that there are 170 lakes dead in New York that will no longer carry any fish or aquatic life. And it occurred to me to ask the question . . . well, how much are the fish worth in these 170 lakes that account for four percent of the lake area in New York? And does it make sense to spend billions of dollars controlling emissions from sources in Ohio and elsewhere if you're talking about very marginal volume of dollar value, either in recreational terms or commercial terms?"

Stockman's words reminded some people of Oscar Wilde's definition of a cynic: a man who knows the price of everything and the value of nothing. This sort of "cost-benefit" analysis suggests that everything, including the experience of an outing at a wilderness lake, has a specific price tag. The people of the United States reject this reasoning. They have supported many costly government programs because they believed that something worthwhile needed to be done.

At the EPA, Reagan administrator Ann Gorsuch worked toward relaxation of pollution-control rules. She declared that acid deposition was too poorly understood for any action to be taken. Environmentalists began to refer to the Reagan administration as an "acid reign." Even with another sort of administration, however, efforts to control acid rain would have caused bitter political conflict in the United States.

Unlike some forms of pollution, acid rain has not been perceived as a major threat to human health. Its effects are subtle and gradual. They are most apparent in rural areas, not in major population centers. Those arguing for pollution controls spoke mostly of dead fish and dying lakes, while their opponents cited the possible impact of control measures on people—through lost jobs and high utility bills for consumers. Furthermore, acid rain was not seen as a national issue but mainly as a problem between two regions of the United States.

As public concern grew, legislation to control acid rain was introduced in Congress. (Between 1981 and 1984 more than three dozen laws were proposed.) The battle lines were drawn. Two alliances developed, one favoring control, one opposed.

The pro-control alliance included elected representatives from the acid rain receptor regions (including New York, New England, and Canada), government natural resource agencies, environmental groups from both the United States and Canada, representatives of the outdoor tourism business from the receptor regions and (to a limited extent) of industries that make scrubbers and other air-pollution-control equipment. The pro-control forces also had the support of many biologists who were aware of the harm caused by acid rain.

These forces wanted acid rain reduced quickly. They emphasized and sometimes exaggerated the most negative aspects of scientific studies, including any preliminary evidence that suggested widespread harm to the environment and to human health. They used the mass media to arouse public opinion and to generate pressure from citizens on their elected representatives.

The anti-control alliance included elected representatives from states where most acid rain originates, as well as representatives of the coal industry and the United Mine Workers union, electric utilities, the mining and auto industries, and industry-supported research institutes. This alliance was determined to avoid change that might hurt them economically. Through the media, in government forums, and in their own publications, they stressed that acid rain was not a problem or, if it was, it was too poorly understood for any action to be taken. They also exaggerated the economic costs of a control program, creating studies that showed huge increases in utility bills and massive losses of miners' jobs.

For example, the electric utility industry claimed that if sulfur dioxide emissions were cut by 40 percent, electric rates in the Midwest would rise at least 18 percent and as much as 63 percent in some cases. The congressional Office of Technology Assessment (OTA) studied the matter and concluded that no consumer would pay more than a 16 percent increase. According to the OTA, the increase would be between 6 and 9 percent in Ohio, Illinois, West Virginia, and Tennessee.

Politically the anti-control forces supported the idea that long-term government-funded research was needed. Through the Electric Power Research Institute (EPRI), utilities actually funded acid rain research. (In one case, EPRI funds enabled University of Vermont botanists to connect acid deposition to forest decline; once this evidence was revealed, the EPRI financial support was not renewed.) The anti-control forces exploited the basic caution of scientists in order to emphasize the unanswered questions about acid deposition. Finally, when a national acid rain control program seemed inevitable, the anti-control forces lobbied to ensure that the costs would fall on consumers, not polluters.

At their most extreme, people opposed to acid rain controls resorted to name-calling. Governor James Rhodes of Ohio—the state burning the most high-sulfur coal—called environmentalists the "birds-and-berries people," and said that they had "latched on to acid rain as a rallying cry for a new wave of environmental hysteria." An Ohio congressman claimed that, "Acid rain is a conspiracy cooked up by the Canadian government in order to sell more electric power to the United States."

More insidious were the distortions of fact found in the testimony and publications of the anti-control forces. In 1980, for example, an EPRI official told a congressional committee, "In EPRI's lake acidification study, we have found three lakes in the Adirondack Mountains of New York which have very different acidities, yet these lakes lie within a few miles of each other and chemistry of the rainfall is the same at all three. Obviously, some factor other than precipitation is responsible for the acidity."

In fact, the EPRI-funded research had shown that the soil characteristics of different watersheds influenced the acidity of the three lakes and that precipitation had caused increased acidity in the most vulnerable lake, Woods Lake. (This study is described on pages 32–34.) Years later the evidence from this research was still misrepresented in information booklets from utilities and in a booklet called *Acid Rain: Answers to Your Questions*, published in 1985 by the Edison Electric Institute, a lobbying group for electric utilities.

This booklet consists mostly of brief quotations from scientific reports, press releases, magazine articles, and other statements about acid rain. It claims to present "a new understanding ... about the sources of atmospheric acidity and the role of acidity in environmental matters," based on a "sampling" of literature. The new understanding is, in brief, that acid rain is not a problem.

To a naive reader the booklet appears authoritative, with its list of more than sixty references. Certain scientists or firms whose research was funded by the utility industry are quoted repeatedly; most quotations are taken out of context from scientific reports that actually expressed concern about acid deposition. In fact, several thousand studies related to acid deposition have been published in the scientific journals of several nations. A random sample of this vast literature would give an understanding of acid rain much different from that conveyed by the relatively few studies selected for inclusion by the Edison Electric Institute. *Acid Rain: Answers to Your Questions* gives the sort of answers a wise citizen expects from a utility lobbying organization.

The Environmental Protection Agency has found its credibility as an environmental watchdog badly eroded by the politics of the acid rain controversy. The EPA relies on scientific research to set policies, but seemed to distort or ignore evidence, much as the anti-control forces did. In 1981 an assistant administrator of the EPA said that three to five more years of study would be needed before regulatory action could be taken. During the following years, reports from the National Academy of Sciences, the Office of Technology Assessment, and the White House Office of Science and Technology Policy agreed that adequate information already existed to start a control effort. Nevertheless, in 1985 EPA administrator Lee Thomas said that the agency was still waiting for a better understanding of the problem.

Spokespersons for the EPA and for the polluters it is empowered to regulate warned about rushing into action before scientific certainty existed. But all sorts of government decisions are based on incomplete information. Senator George Mitchell of Maine said, "The argument that we have to wait until we have the complete answer to every part of the problem is the argument most used by people who want inaction, want no action. And were we to wait for that day, it will be your grandson and my grandson who will be discussing the issue then. Human affairs do not lend themselves, and never have lent themselves, to the approach that you have to have a precise scientific answer to every conceivable question that exists before you take any legislative action."

The Environmental Protection Agency is responsible for enforcing the Clean Air Act, which was passed by

Congress in 1970 and amended in 1977. The law does not mention acid rain but empowers the EPA to regulate sulfur dioxide and nitrogen oxides; it also has provisions for regulating pollution that crosses state or national boundaries. Several provisions give the EPA authority to tackle the problem of acid rain, but some loopholes exist that the EPA has used as an excuse for inaction.

In 1980, when the EPA allowed several midwestern utilities to increase sulfur dioxide emissions, New York State petitioned the agency to have this permission withdrawn because of the likelihood that increased acid rain would fall on New York and Canada. In 1981 the EPA granted New York a hearing but allowed no testimony on acid rain. The reason, declared the agency, was that it had no authority to consider acid rain, because the Clean Air Act set limits on sulfur dioxide, not on acids that formed from it.

Nevertheless, in 1982, when a bill was proposed in Congress specifically to empower the EPA to regulate acid rain, the agency argued against it. An EPA administrator testified, "Given the vigorous prevention and control program already in place in this country, probably the best in the world, the question before us is whether an additional program is necessary to protect against more distant effects. This is why a study program is needed, and why the Clean Air Act gives us the confidence so that we need not move precipitously."

The EPA certainly could not be accused of acting in haste. Four years after New York had petitioned for a hearing and two years after the hearing ended, the agency still had made no decision. In March 1984 New York sued the EPA for dereliction of duty. Several environmental organizations and all northeastern states joined in the suit. In 1985 a federal district judge ruled in their favor, ordering the EPA to act against acid rain. But the agency appealed to the Court of Appeals for the District of Columbia, which in 1986 dismissed the suit, saying that agencies cannot make rules without public notice or without giving affected parties an opportunity to comment.

Meanwhile, another suit against the EPA had been filed in late 1985. It was based on the agency's failure to revise its standards for sulfur dioxide, as it was legally required to do in 1980 and every five years thereafter. "Once again we have to sue the EPA for not doing its job," said Robert Abrams, New York's attorney general. Joining in the suit were New Hampshire, Massachusetts, Vermont, Rhode Island, Minnesota, and several environmental groups, including the Natural Resources Defense Council and the Environmental Defense Fund. Environmental groups also filed several other suits against the EPA, based on provisions of the Clean Air Act.

During the Reagan administration, relations between the United States and Canada grew more strained over the acidic pollutants blowing northward. Canadians were encouraged in the fall of 1985 when Drew Lewis, President Reagan's special envoy to Canada on this matter, said, "It seems to me that saying sulfur does not cause acid rain is the same as saying that smoking does not cause lung cancer."

Hopes for meaningful action were soon dashed, however, when Lewis made his recommendations: a five-year, $5 billion research program on cleaner ways to

"THIS IS CERTAINLY A PROBLEM. LET'S STUDY IT FOR ANOTHER YEAR."

Editorial cartoonists expressed the truth of the matter—that steps toward control, not more study, were needed and overdue.

burn coal. In other words, more study, and no steps taken actually to reduce emissions reaching Canada. A spokesperson for the Canadian Coalition on Acid Rain, a political lobbying group, said, "There is no progress at all as far as the basic issue is concerned."

In 1986 President Reagan and Canadian Prime Minister Mulroney endorsed the recommendation that the United States would step up its research. In 1987 President Reagan said he would seek $2.5 billion over five years for research on coal burning. His proposal was widely assailed as a delaying tactic. Robert Abrams, the attorney general of New York, said, "It is especially unwise and wasteful for the Government to spend huge amounts of money to develop emission control technology when we already know what causes acid rain and we already have the technology to control it."

The Canadian government itself had for several years been criticized for weak regulation of pollutants. When action finally came, it was motivated in part by the hope that a good example would spur change in the United States.

In 1985 Canada launched a control program aimed to cut sulfur dioxide emissions by half within ten years. In 1986 Ontario took more dramatic action involving the four sources that emitted 80 percent of that province's sulfur dioxide. These were coal-fired power plants of Ontario Hydro, two copper smelters at Sudbury, and an iron-processing plant. Ontario's legislation required these sources to eliminate two-thirds of their sulfur dioxide emissions by 1994. Flagrant violations of this law could bring fines of up to a half million dollars a day or jail sentences for corporate officials.

This strengthened Canada's case against the United States, the source of more than half of the acid deposition in Canada. James Bradley, Ontario's Minister of the Environment, said, "Our U.S. neighbours must follow suit, or Ontario's sensitive lakes will continue to die. Even if Canada cut sulfur dioxide emissions to zero, these lakes still could not withstand continued acidification from the United States."

Several states, including New York and Minnesota, also passed acid rain control laws. And, if pro-control forces needed another good example, there was Japan. Between 1970 and 1975 Japan reduced its sulfur emissions by half, largely by installing more than a thousand scrubbers on coal-burning power plants. Japan has since reduced sulfur emissions still further. West Germany also took belated action to reduce the pollutants that harmed its forests. A Canadian environmental official said in 1987, "The U.S. is out of step with other Western industrialized countries, almost all of which have targets to reduce emissions by 40 to 60 percent by the middle of the next decade."

The pro-control forces in the United States grew increasingly hopeful that the acid rain policy paralysis would finally end. At an acid rain conference held in late 1986, David Wooley, an assistant attorney general of New York, said, "There is a growing frustration and

In the mid-1980s Canada took action to reduce acidic emissions from its major sources, including the Inco Superstack at Sudbury.

contempt for EPA's foot-dragging, and Congress or the courts will sweep it aside in the next year or so. If Congress doesn't act the courts will."

He warned that an acid rain control law should give the EPA "no discretion." Without strong presidential support, the EPA, like most federal regulatory agencies, regulates only when the pressures to do so are greater than the pressures that favor inaction or retrenchment.

In 1987 the anti-control forces were encouraged by an interim report of the National Acid Precipitation Assessment Program. Established by Congress in 1980, this research program had spent $300 million on studies of acid deposition. The quality of the research was good, but many scientists were surprised at the report, which claimed there wasn't much to worry about. Only a small percentage of lakes in the Northeast were acidified, it said, and "a significant increase in the number of acidic lakes is unlikely to occur over the next few decades." The report's summary also claimed there was little damage to forests, no damage to crops, and "no demonstrated effects" on human health from acid rain.

The report provoked not just predictable criticism from environmental groups but also criticism from scientists, including individuals who had conducted some of the research. Several scientists said they could not comment publicly because they feared they would lose federal funds for their studies.

Although the four-volume, 900-page report included findings of harm done by acid rain, its 36-page summary—all that most members of Congress and journalists would read—gave an exceptionally rosy view of the problem. "It is the way things are put, the order they are in, the way they are phrased," said Gene Likens, who found the summary "rather highly politicized."

Canadian biologist David Schindler said, "It looks like a deliberate effort to downplay the effects." Schindler and other aquatic biologists pointed out how data were presented in a way that underestimated damage to lakes. The report used pH 5 as its cutoff point for defining an acidic lake. David Schindler and other scientists said that damage to aquatic life could be detected at pH 6, and that most fish species stopped reproducing at a pH of 5.3 to 5.6. At pH 5 nearly half of a lake's life is usually gone.

Director of the research program J. Laurence Kulp said that pH 5 was chosen because below that level sport fish start to show dramatic effects. Harm to insects and other aquatic life was ignored because it did not lower the *economic* value of a body of water. He claimed that the report was a "state-of-the-art science document," but many scientists called it a startling misrepresentation of their understanding of acid deposition.

People advocating control of acid rain were encouraged by the results of an economic study released in 1987. Economists at a firm based in Washington, D.C., called Management Information Services (which had received no outside funding for its work) applied computer models to the provisions of different acid rain control bills under consideration in the Senate and House of Representatives. For the first time, estimates were made of the net economic impact of acid rain abatement, rather than focusing only on the estimated annual costs of $4 billion to $9 billion.

According to this study, after factoring in expected

job and sales losses in such industries as coal mining, the net gain for the United States would range from $7.5 billion to $13 billion. Depending on the final legislation, there would be a net gain of 100,000 to 194,000 jobs.

The economic study took the negative effects of control legislation into account, including some to which no dollar value can be assigned: "It is little solace to an unemployed coal miner to know of jobs opening up in another part of the state, for computer specialists or electrical engineers." But the report by Management Information Services concluded, "Far from hurting U.S. industry, acid rain control legislation, through large

A major concern about changes brought by acid rain control was its economic impact on regions where high-sulfur coal is mined.

purchases of capital equipment and supporting goods and services it will generate, will provide a much needed shot-in-the-arm for many anemic U.S. manufacturing, capital goods, machine tool, iron and steel and related industries."

This study did not, of course, reduce opposition from anti-control forces. Electric utilities and coal companies financed a new lobbying group called Citizens for Sensible Control of Acid Rain, which spent $3 million in 1986 alone. Its name suggested that its backers expected an acid rain control law, and sought to make it as weak as possible. But opinion polls showed that the American people found acid rain unacceptable and were willing to pay for its cleanup.

The crux of the acid rain cleanup problem has always been its considerable cost and who should bear it. Pro-control forces have learned that a *fair* law—one that requires polluters to pay—is not politically viable. Legislation that eases the financial burden on polluters has a better chance of passage. In 1986 a bill with this provision attracted 167 co-sponsors in the House of Representatives. It never reached the House floor, but most of its provisions were included in several acid rain control bills that were introduced to the One-hundredth Congress, which convened in January 1987.

The most promising legislation calls for a 10-million-ton reduction in sulfur dioxide emissions in ten years. Although most scientists recommend a cut of at least 12 million tons, the costs of achieving the additional reduction would be high, as would the political resistance. The proposed legislation would also allow each state to decide for itself how to achieve sulfur dioxide reductions, whether through scrubbers, fuel switching, fuel washing, use of modern coal-burning plants, or a combination of steps.

The proposed legislation also spreads the cost of compliance around somewhat, by limiting the increase in consumer electricity rates to 10 percent. Any increase beyond that would be financed by a nationwide tax on consumption of electricity generated from fossil fuels. However, this tax would not be the same in all states. It would be linked to pollution levels, and states with already-low sulfur dioxide emissions would pay little. This won support from westerners who resented paying midwestern states to clean up their power plants.

The pro-control forces hope that an acid rain control law with these provisions will be enacted before the One-hundredth Congress ceases work in 1988, or soon after the Reagan administration ends. Success will not come easily, however, because powerful senators and members of Congress who represent the interests of high-sulfur coal mining and the automobile industry can keep legislation from coming to a vote.

Once launched, a federal program for decreasing acid rain will take most of a decade to achieve its full effect on emissions. Disturbing change will touch the coal industry. Electric utilities will have to reevaluate their fuel choices and plans for new plants. People will pay somewhat more for electricity. The high-sulfur coal industry may suffer while manufacturers of coal scrubbers prosper.

These costs and benefits of acid rain controls are much easier to quantify than the benefits downwind. Although the damage caused by acid deposition is real, much of it has been difficult to isolate or to express in dollars. Many of the benefits of declining acidity will also be subtle and gradual. They will be measured first in rising precipitation pH, then in easier breathing for people with asthma, in revived forest growth, in loons and black ducks successfully rearing their young, and in the resurgence of salmon and striped bass populations.

Resolution of the acid rain problem may bring other benefits to the United States. The policy stalemate has been costly. It has severely strained relations with Canada. It has pitted the Northeast against the Midwest. To an unusual extent it has allowed political and economic interests to ignore and distort the best wisdom scientists have made available. It has revealed the Environmental Protection Agency—at least the EPA under the Reagan administration—to be a guardian more of utilities and the coal industry than of the welfare of the general public.

In the late twentieth century, the United States faces many complex problems that have to be tackled with incomplete knowledge. It cannot continue to stall for time. The American people need a sense that their leaders and institutions can solve problems, not just store them for the future. The benefits of a strong national acid rain control program may not only revive trout and trees, but also help restore peoples' hope and confidence that their government can grapple with the challenges of today and tomorrow.

Further
Reading

Most of the periodicals listed below continue to publish articles about acid rain; see recent issues for the most up-to-date information. In addition, the *Acid Precipitation Digest* is available by subscription from the Acid Rain Information Clearinghouse, a project of the Center for Environmental Information, Inc., 33 S. Washington Street, Rochester, New York 14608.

ALVO, ROBERT. "Lost Loons of the Northern Lakes." *Natural History,* September 1986, pp. 58–65.

BALZHIZER, RICHARD, AND YEAGER, KURT. "Coal-fired Power Plants for the Future." *Scientific American,* September 1987, pp. 100–107.

BOYLE, ROBERT, AND BOYLE, R. ALEXANDER. *Acid Rain.* New York: Schocken Books, 1983.

COWLING, ELLIS. "Acid Precipitation in Historical Perspective." *Environmental Science & Technology,* vol. 16, no. 2 (1982), pp. 110–123.

GAURI, K. L., AND HOLDREN, G., JR. "Pollutant Effects on Stone Monuments." *Environmental Science & Technology,* vol. 15, no. 4 (1981), pp. 386–390.

GOULD, ROY. *Going Sour: Science and Politics of Acid Rain.* Boston: Birkhauser, 1985.

LABASTILLE, ANNE. "Acid Rain: How Great a Menace?" *National Geographic,* November 1981, pp. 650–681.

LIKENS, GENE, *et al.* "Acid Rain." *Scientific American,* October 1979, pp. 43–51.

LINTHURST, RICK, ED. *Direct and Indirect Effects of Acidic Deposition on Vegetation.* Boston: Butterworths, 1984.

LUOMA, JON. "Forests Are Dying but Is Acid Rain to Blame?" *Audubon,* March 1987, pp. 36–51.

———. *Troubled Skies, Troubled Waters: The Story of Acid Rain.* New York: Viking Press, 1984.

NATIONAL ACADEMY OF SCIENCES. *Acid Deposition: Atmospheric Processes in Eastern North America.* Washington, D.C.: National Academy Press, 1983.

NATIONAL ACID PRECIPITATION ASSESSMENT PROGRAM. *Interim Assessment: The Causes and Effects of Acidic Deposition.* 4 vols. Washington, D.C.: U.S. Government Printing Office, 1987.

OSTMANN, ROBERT, JR. *Acid Rain: A Plague upon the Waters.* Minneapolis: Dillon Press, 1982.

PAWLICK, THOMAS. *A Killing Rain: The Global Threat of Acid Precipitation.* San Francisco: Sierra Club Books, 1984.

RAHN, KENNETH, AND LOWENTHAL, DOUGLAS. "The Acid Rain Whodunnit." *Natural History,* July 1986, pp. 62–65.

ROBERTS, LESLIE. "Federal Report on Acid Rain Draws Criticism." *Science,* 18 September 1987, pp. 1404–1406.

ROTH, PHILIP, *et al. The American West's Acid Rain Test.* Washington, D.C.: World Resources Institute, 1985.

SCHINDLER, DAVID, *et al.* "Long-term Ecosystem Stress: The Effects of Years of Experimental Acidification on a Small Lake." *Science,* 21 June 1985, pp. 1395–1401.

———. "Natural Sources of Acid Neutralizing Capacity in Low Alkalinity Lakes of the Precambrian Shield." *Science,* 16 May 1986, pp. 844–847.

———. "Effects of Acid Rain on Freshwater Ecosystems." *Science,* 8 January 1988, pp. 149–157.

STREETS, DAVID, *et al.* "Selected Strategies to Reduce Acidic Deposition in the U.S." *Environmental Science & Technology,* vol. 17, no. 8 (1983), pp. 474–485.

SWEDISH MINISTRY OF AGRICULTURE. *Acidification Today and Tomorrow.* Stockholm, Sweden: Ministry of Agriculture, 1982.

TOMLINSON, GEORGE. "Air Pollutants and Forest Decline." *Environmental Science & Technology,* vol. 17, no. 6 (1983), pp. 246–256.

U.S. CONGRESS, OFFICE OF TECHNOLOGY ASSESSMENT. *Acid Rain and Transported Air Pollutants: Implications for Public Policy.* Washington, D.C.: Office of Technology Assessment, 1984.

U.S. ENVIRONMENTAL PROTECTION AGENCY, OFFICE OF RESEARCH AND DEVELOPMENT. *The Acid Deposition Phenomenon and Its Effects.* 2 vols. Washington, D.C.: Environmental Protection Agency, 1983.

WETSTONE, GREGORY, AND FOSTER, SARAH. "Acid Precipitation: What Is It Doing to Our Forests?" *Environment,* May 1983, pp. 10–12, 38–40.

WHITE, JAMES, ED. *Acid Rain: The Relationship Between Sources and Receptors.* New York: Elsevier Science Publishing Co., 1987.

YANARELLA, E., AND IHARA, R., EDS. *The Acid Rain Debate: Scientific, Economic, and Political Dimensions.* Boulder, Colorado: Westview Press, 1985.

Index

Asterisk (*) indicates illustration